SECOND ED

SELLING GRAPHIC DESIGN

BY **DON SPARKMAN** • FOREWORD BY **ED GOLD**

Allworth Press, New York

Published by Allworth Press, an imprint of Allworth Communications, Inc.
10 East 23rd Street, Suite 210, New York, NY 10010

Library of Congress Catalog Number: 98-72767
ISBN: 1-58115-017-2

Cover and text design:

Don Sparkman
President
Sparkman + Associates, Inc.

Printed in Canada

To my Catherine, who knows how cold
cold-calling can be.

INSIDE

THE BUSINESS OF SELLING GRAPHIC DESIGN

If you're in business, you're in the business of selling. If you're in the business of graphic design, you're in the business of selling your aesthetic solutions, your marketing insights, your technical expertise, and, most importantly, yourself. You also have an obligation to yourself, your employees, your profession, and your colleagues to sell those solutions that make a profit for your business, adhere to the ethical standards of behavior set down by your peers, and cause as little damage to the environment as possible.

This is a tall order. Unfortunately, few graphic designers are either educated or psychologically prepared to deal with all the complex factors that go into becoming the type of effective salesperson who can skillfully balance all these demands.

A large majority of designers seem to be under the curious belief that all they have to do to bring in plenty of projects is to create terrific designs. I say "curious" because these same designers are also consumers who are well aware that the quality of a product or service is only one small factor in whether or not they choose to buy it.

To begin with, they first have to want that product or service. Notice I didn't say "need" that product or service. There's a difference.

When a pipe bursts in my basement during the middle of the night, I don't have to be told that I need a plumber. And I'll take any plumber I can get who is willing to go wading at four o'clock in the morning.

I happen to want a Mercedes convertible. I certainly don't need one. But I can almost guarantee that once these words are published I'll be getting a call from my friendly local Mercedes dealer with an offer I probably won't be able to refuse.

Graphic designers are much more in the position of a Mercedes salesperson than of a plumber. Anyone can see that if the burst pipe isn't fixed quickly, the house might soon become valuable only to fishes. But most people are quite willing to get from one place to another without the aid of several tons of German engineering.

While designers may see very clearly how badly the world needs their design solutions, unfortunately almost all of their potential clients have to be convinced that, without the help of a professional graphic designer, their business or institution will soon be in lots of trouble. Designers often have to create a "want" where none exists.

Having established a "want," designers next have to convince a client that the client's business goals can best be achieved by hiring their design firm, most of the time in spite of the fact that there may be less expensive people to hire.

Finally, designers have to persuade their clients that the design solution proposed is the best one to achieve the clients' goals. This is never easy, because there are few quantifiable ways to measure the success or lack thereof of a graphic design. In fact, graphic design is one of the few professions where its practitioners find themselves constantly arguing with the very people upon whom their livelihood depends. If not handled with a great deal of tact and diplomacy, this livelihood might quickly disappear.

I have known Don Sparkman for many years and have always been struck by his no-nonsense approach to both the art and the business of graphic design. He has always clearly grasped the essential truth that, to spend his days doing what he wants—producing wonderful design solutions—he has to spend an equal amount of time managing his business intelligently.

The key to the success of a graphic design business does not lie in the ability to produce excellent design solutions, but in getting someone to pay to have these solutions reach the public. Not just any someone, but someone who is willing to allow the designer to do the best work he or she is capable of.

To sell graphic design, a designer must be knowledgeable about every aspect of design, design history, and the technology of design, which changes almost every day.

In just the past few years, more and more designers have begun to accept the reality that somehow their future and the future of their design firms will be linked to their understanding of the Internet and their ability to control and design for the Web.

---

*Designers often
have to create a "want"
where none exists.*

For the time being and, most likely, for many more years, designers who know how to get the most out of the Web and also know how to communicate their knowledge without using the incomprehensible jargon that so permeates the world of the Web, will have an enormous edge over competitors who do not.

Designers also have to learn how to seek out those clients who will be a help, not a hindrance, to their business. They have to learn how to make potential clients aware that they exist at all and then convince these clients to hire them in the face of tremendous competition from other individuals and design firms. They have to learn how to persuade clients to trust them and their design solutions. Finally, they have to learn how to buy electronic and publishing services intelligently so that they don't throw away their clients' hard-earned trust.

In this book, Don covers all these subjects and much more. In the thirty-some years that Don has been selling his company's services, he has learned more about the complex process of selling graphic design than any designer I have ever met.

This book is must reading for any designer who has ever found himself or herself wondering what it takes to produce the best work he or she is capable of doing and see that this work actually gets produced and is profitable.

ED GOLD

Ed Gold is a professor in the School of Communications Design, which is part of the Yale Gordon College of Liberal Arts, University of Baltimore. He is the author of The Business of Graphic Design *(Watson-Guptill, 1995).*

INTRODUCTION

THE HARD-SELL

I'm sure you've heard of the school of hard knocks. This is about the school of hard sell, because selling is hard. Common sense is the thread binding these pages together.

If you are an account executive, graphic designer, or an entrepreneur, this book will give you a sense of where the business of graphic design started and where it's headed. There may be things here that will reaffirm what you already know. The book was written to help you avoid mistakes, not miss opportunities, and close sales. You'll learn how to target the right clients, network, and write effective proposals. Best of all, you'll see graphic design as a lucrative business opportunity.

This book is about selling. Print, at this printing, is still the biggest medium and will probably coexist with the Internet as the most portable means of communicating effectively. In this book, I have addressed selling on the Internet with broad strokes. The World Wide Web is a frontier that is constantly changing. If you want to become a guru in this industry, I suggest attending some of the many seminars offered and, best of all, befriending a designer who can address your questions in the context of design, not programming. This is very important because there are many self-proclaimed experts in the field, often diguising their lack of design ability with their technical knowledge.

All of us are in sales. In every profession, we are selling ourselves. Whether it's to the public or to our employer, we are selling. Now the hard part. Salespeople are only paid for what they sell. No sales, no pay. Your company's investment in you as a salesperson is much smaller than its investment in graphic designers. Designers require training, expensive equipment such as computer systems, and office overhead.

Are you a salesperson or a professional salesperson? There's a difference. A professional knows the profession inside and out. In this age of the new electronic design technology, you have a lot more to learn than your predecessors ever did. But, on the other hand, you have a tremendous opportunity to become a valuable asset to your prospective clients. In many cases, they are not knowledgeable in the technology, and they are afraid to let anyone know how little they know. You can be their greatest ally.

You can turn a rainy day into the best selling day of your career.

Every negative has an equal if not stronger positive. You can turn a rainy day into the best selling day of your career. Why? Because your prospects are all in their offices trying to stay dry. This makes them more accessible to you. You can bring a breath of fresh air to them by being cheery and thoughtful. I remember a very successful printing saleswoman who made it a point to bring donuts to her first appointment.

In this book, we'll start off with a little history of graphic design and printing. You need an overview to understand why we are in such an exciting era. You're selling graphic design, but printing is the end-result, and you need to know as much about printing as graphic design.

If your company buys illustration, photography, prepress services, paper, printing, or Internet services, you'll learn how to get the most for your company's dollar. There are ways of turning low budgets into highly successful projects. There are tricks known by the pros that can make you look like a hero. And let's face it, you don't need many mistakes to become a loser.

Whether you work for an advertising agency, a design firm, a Web design firm, or for yourself, the rules are the same. It's unusual, in the current economy, for anyone to be able to buy with total freedom. Bids are the rule, no longer the exception. In the past, buyers could sole-source their work. That meant they could use your company without getting three bids. That's not true any longer. This book will show you how to prepare *your* ultimate proposal. You will still need to do your homework, though. The more homework you do, the better your chances.

Each proposal is a unique blend of your company's capabilities, your understanding of the project, and the quotation. The price alone does not guarantee a winning proposal. If three prices are close or equal, the proposal's structure and substance come into play.

Today, the media your company works in isn't as important as the results of your sales efforts. Your company can be the world's answer to high-tech graphic design and super-savvy in cyberspace, but with no customers, there's no business, no remuneration, no reason to come to work, etc.

Several years ago I had a meeting in my conference room with the principals of two other design firms. We were meeting as an advisory committee to the local art directors' club. When the business part of the meeting ended we began talking about business in general. Both of the other companies were ahead of mine in technology. They had more sophisticated software and expensive hardware.

We talked about the business climate and more importantly, clients. There's a large bookcase on the far wall of my conference room where I display our work. The majority of the pieces are high-end and full color. I commented that I believed that "design" was the most important thing my company did and that, while also important, electronics didn't seem to impress my clients.

One of my guests shook his head, motioned toward the bookcase and said, "That's easy for you to say, we don't have Fortune 500 clients like you do!"

I nodded politely, wondering if he would later analyze what he had just said to me. Or would he always believe that better design doesn't bring better clients?

If you are selling shoes or cars, it only makes sense to want to sell the best product available. If you are selling graphic design, you should be selling the best graphic design; anything else your company does should only support this function.

HISTORY

It's not just where we're going,
but where we've been.

CHAPTER 1

GRAPHIC DESIGN, TYPOGRAPHY PREPRESS, THE INTERNET: THEN AND NOW

To understand graphic design today, we need to know a little about the recent developments in the field. I'm not going to take you back to the days of cave drawings, and I'm not going to bore you with a lesson in art history. If you're over forty and have been in the field, skim this chapter. This is for you beginners.

The Early Years

In the first half of the twentieth century, commercial artists/ graphic designers were primarily typesetters and printers. Some were illustrators, but they were totally different from people who designed pages. Until sometime in the 1950s, graphic design was little more than an embellishment of the printed word. Examples can be seen in the old stationers' books, which gave the buyers of printing strict and rigid formats for their letterheads, envelopes, and business cards.

In this same time frame, advertising design and illustration lived a separate life from graphic design. Advertising agencies used wonderful illustrations, hand lettering, and creative borders to sell everything from underwear to fine cars. What set the two industries apart? Money. For most companies, corporate identity was not even a glimmer in their eyes.

Typography in the Early Years

Let's look at typography in the 1950s. Typesetters were usually a part of a printing plant. Printing was primarily letterpress, meaning that the printing plate came directly in contact with the paper running through the press. There were independent typographers, but they were the exceptions to the rule. As the communications industry started to grow in the 1960s, typographers opened up trade shops at an accelerated rate.

At this time, typesetting was becoming more specialized, and so was printing. As with other industries, specialization became the response to complexity. We've seen this in medicine and law. No longer are there many general practitioners. There is just too much information to digest. The same has been true of the entire graphic arts industry. With the entrance of total digital technology, the entire printing industry, from graphic design to the waterless presses, has become so complex that specialization has become the rule.

The Beginnings of Design as an Industry

Let's look at the sixties. Things were changing. A few true graphic design firms were starting to spring up in metropolitan areas around the country. These companies were primarily in New York, Chicago, Dallas, Houston, Los Angeles, and San Francisco.

In 1966, the typical scenario went something like this: A printing salesman (never a woman) would visit his favorite graphic design firm. The salesman would present his customer's requirements to the designer. The designer would produce a hand-crafted layout in pastels or markers and explain the rationale behind the graphic solution or layout to the printing salesman. The designer would put the layout in a plain envelope. The printing salesman would then affix his company's label to it and go to his client's office. This worked well for a while. Graphic design appeared to be an in-house function of the printer.

As more and more design firms cropped up, the corporate buyer became more sophisticated. Good graphics were emerging everywhere. When the buyer felt the design did not suit his needs, it was rejected. This put the printing salesman in the position of having to return to the designer with a rejected layout. The designer may have followed the printing salesman's instructions to the letter, but the instructions may not have been an exact interpretation of what the buyer wanted. Something as simple as the client's disliking a color could cause a layout to be rejected.

When it became apparent that the designer had to be paid for a good faith effort when the buyer refused to accept the work, the printing salesman began to question his role as a broker in this new era of graphic design. It wasn't long before the printer introduced the designer to the client. The designer agreed to protect the printer's interests, while working directly with the client. This took the liability away from the printer, and thus graphic design became an industry—and a growing industry at that.

Design's Yellow Submarine Era

In the mid 1960s, "corporate identity" made its major debut. There were companies who had developed strong identities much earlier, but for the most part, they were the elite. They were the AT&Ts, IBMs, and GMs of the country. In the seventies, every company felt it had to have a corporate identity.

This was called the "Yellow Submarine" era of graphic design. Push Pin Studio's Milton Glaser and Seymour Chwast were the renaissance men of design. Other greats, like Massimo Vignelli of Unimark, Paul Rand of Westinghouse, and Saul Bass made the late sixties and seventies a highly charged time for the graphic design industry. In the sixties, the Beatles introduced the music that set the stage for this exciting time. Whether you loved or hated the seventies, they changed our lives forever.

Hot Type

As the number of design firms increased, typesetting companies continued to grow both in number and size. In the 1970s, typesetting was done using the traditional Linotype machine, which used hot metal to make up lines and blocks of text type. Paper repros (a reproduction proof) were produced from this type on a proofing press. There was an art to pulling repros so that the sheets were consistently perfect.

With the advent of offset printing, printers required camera-ready art. The repro was now ready for the printer to photograph with a copy-camera. After the repro was photographed, a film negative was created. This negative would later be exposed to a photosensitized aluminum plate. "Offset" meant that the plate passed the ink onto a rubber blanket which then transferred the image to a sheet of paper.

The Business of Design

While the look of graphic design was changing, so was the business. Graphic design firms were brokers for the most part. That is, they bought typography from a typesetter and billed the client, adding a mark-up or handling charge based on a percentage of the actual cost. Many design firms also bought the printing for a project and marked it up as well. All in all, this was a very lucrative way of doing business.

The shoe was now on the other foot. The printer's customer was now the designer. This lasted well into the eighties when the nation's economy heated up. Some design firms even got into the typesetting business and bought expensive equipment. Every angle of making money was explored by graphic designers.

Unfortunately, what goes up must come down. Clients with great track records and proven credit were suddenly going out of business or, at the least, turning into slow payers. The designers were often left with the big bills from the printers and typesetters. Brokering was dangerous business for small design firms without much working capital behind them.

Cold type was the next logical step in the development of typography. Simply put, cold type is the opposite of hot metal. It is a photographic process using photographic paper, which is much more stable than the older repro sheets that used ink. Set photographically, the characters were so sharp that they could be enlarged many times and still look crisp. This was in marked contrast to hot type. The hot type repro, enlarged only slightly, showed the imperfections due to ink on paper.

Design Joins Technology

In the late 1980s, computers were introduced to graphic designers. There were a few firms who had entered the electronic era earlier. They borrowed heavily to equip themselves with the large design workstations from companies like Lightspeed, DuPont, and Crosfield. These design firms took the first jolts of what heavy capital investment could do to a small company—some survived.

> *You can have speed, lots of memory, or an inexpensive price tag. You can have any two, but not all three.*

When the Macintosh was developed for graphic design, it wasn't long before great new software was being announced monthly to enhance the capabilities of these affordable computers. They were slow, but they were cheap when compared to the earlier systems. And that brings in an equation that is still true today. You can have speed, lots of memory, or an inexpensive price tag. You can have any two, but not all three.

Today, graphic designers use computers, and, for the most part, they do not use typesetters. Your client's copy on floppy disks can be imported directly into the computer. The Macintosh can take IBM programs such as WordPerfect or Microsoft Word. This means your client's copy will not have to be retyped. It's amazing that in the last thirty years of graphic design, designers have used computers for only the last five or six years.

The Bullet in the Head of an Industry

The computer was dismissed by the professional typographers as a poor alternative to fine typography. And this was true in the beginning. The early programs weren't sophisticated. The typefaces were poor imitations of the typography used by the professionals. The letter-spacing and word-spacing were poor.

Typographers should have realized that anything with this much promise could and would be improved.

The typographers felt that the personal computer was neither a threat nor an ally. Little did they know what was coming. If they had thought about technology in general, they would have realized that anything with this much promise could and would be improved.

Remember the first digital wristwatches? I know someone who paid a thousand dollars for one of the first ones. Now you can get one for under five dollars. This same person also paid a thousand dollars for the first cordless phone, and now everybody has one. This is not saying that you should wait indefinitely to buy into new technology, but you should not dismiss it as too crude or too expensive.

The Next Disaster

The evolution wasn't going to stop here. Printers realized that the image-setting equipment was cheap in contrast to buying the printing presses. They jumped on the bandwagon. Why not generate their own film? And it didn't take them long to realize that they could cut their personnel in the prepress area of their operations.

There are still many service bureaus who are just now reacting to this next change. Some have been smart and let printers buy their operations along with hiring their employees. This was perfect for the printers too because they were instantly involved in the technology. No growing pains or slow learning curves were necessary.

Enter Cyberspace

The computer is to design, now, as was the paint brush to the impressionists. Not only is design for print composed on the computer, but so is animation for films and commercials as well as incredible special effects.

Now the Internet is the rage. Created as a survival tool in case of a war or some other disaster, what scientists developed as a national security communication system is now the Worldwide Web. Those same scientists couldn't begin to imagine the Internet as it is now and will be in the near future.

Designers are capitalizing on the need for clients' eye-catching graphics on "home pages" to entice "surfers" to visit them. This area of design is exciting, not just because it is a new outlet for talent, but it is a new medium for sending files to printers and full-color print layouts to clients.

Technology has become the friend of the designer. I've watched some of the great names in design bash the computer only to embrace it later and claim to be one of the founding fathers. Computers don't produce poor designs. In fact, computers don't design. They're simply another tool in the designer's toolbox, with endless possibilities.

OPENING THE DOOR

It's not enough to just knock,
you have to get in.

CHAPTER 2

ZEROING IN ON THE RIGHT CLIENTS

Sounds easy. Just get out the phone book. Almost anyone can get clients if they try hard enough. Someone out there will click with your personality. It's the law of probabilities. But, let's face it, effective sales are planned.

The first step is to analyze the company you're working for. *If you are the company then do some of the same soul-searching.* You need to sell what your company is capable of producing. I suggest that you review the type of work the present staff of designers has produced. Many companies exhibit work that previous employees have produced. The current design team may have different strengths and weaknesses.

Meet with the Creative Director or Art Director to learn his or her perception of where the company is going. If possible, meet with all designers to review their individual portfolios. When you ask them to show you their book, let them know you're interested in their work.

After that, meet with the principal or principals of your company with a list of important questions. Here are some basics, but feel free to tailor your questions to your company. Your questions will also generate ideas and responses from those above you, and this could help them develop goals they hadn't previously been aware of.

Marketing is a team effort. The following questions will define your role as part of the team.

1. What are your company's sales goals? In order to know what's reasonable, you should ask what sales were the year before.

2. Who are your company's clients? You need to know current clients as well as ones the company doesn't work with anymore. You need to know if you should avoid anyone on the inactive client list, such as slow-payers and no-payers. Ask what current accounts may be capable of giving out more work and what accounts might need revisiting.

3. What types of new accounts does your company want? If the answer is unclear, it will be up to you to set up a strategy. There are some very strong emerging growth industries. Healthcare, environmental, computer hardware, and software industries are strong now, and it appears that they will continue to be. If real estate is dead as a doornail, stay away from it.

4. What company promotional materials are available to you? Is there an advertising budget? What is company policy on client lunches and other promotional expenses?

5. Are designers available for out-of-office meetings? You need to know that if you have a complicated project, you can have a designer present. This is important because, if you are not a designer, you might not ask all of the right questions. If the answer is *no,* you can try to have the clients meet in your offices.

6. Look at your company's latest proposals. Are they professional and impressive? What has been the success ratio? If you are not able to judge them, read chapter 8, "Writing Your Winning Proposal." A good proposal isn't the *only* factor in getting a project, but it can be very important. You need all of the ammunition you can get.

Many companies still rely on proposals that are not designed well. Their content may be good, but they don't look as good as they could. Make sure a designer has designed your proposal. It may be the first thing a potential client sees from your company.

7. How many layouts are produced for one project? Some companies only show one concept. Others show several. You need to know what you can promise a client.

8. What are normal schedules for various projects? You need to give a prospective client a realistic schedule. Make a list of simple to complex jobs and assign a normal working schedule to each of them.

9. Does your company charge for overtime? Some companies do and some don't. If your company does charge a premium, how is the rate determined? Is it time-and-a-half or double time? If there is no charge for overtime, you can use this as a sales tool.

10. Does your company have regular staff meetings? If it doesn't, you should set a sales meeting schedule. The last thing you need is to work in a vacuum. The company has to be a team or you are going to be the loser. I once worked in sales for a company that had their entire design staff threatening to quit because I was such a free-spirited salesperson. I was very young then, and I didn't realize that I needed these designers more than they thought they needed me. You have to keep the lines of communication open, and that is work.

11. Who estimates on projects? It can vary from company to company, so you need to know how the process works. It is important that you have a grasp of what average projects cost, just so you can talk intelligently with prospective clients. That's not to say you're going to give verbal prices. It gives you a chance to know if a project is out of the question.

12. What equipment is used by your company? You need to know what hardware and software is currently being used by the design staff. This isn't as important as the work your company produces, but it is value added in the eyes of your client.

13. Are the work samples in a central location? You should file all samples so that you know where to find different jobs. After all, you want to tailor your portfolio to the type of account you're soliciting. If it's not being done, you should make it company policy to require a minimum of twenty-five samples of each finished piece. If your company manages printing or buys it, this is fairly easy.

14. If you are on commission, what happens if your company is too busy to accept more work? This is a legitimate question. It's your job to keep the company in the black with good billings, so it's also up to the company to keep you in the black. I personally don't believe in sales commissions for design account executives. They either sell or they don't. And I want to be able to turn them off when we're too busy to take more work but not busy enough to hire more people.

What Is the Right Account?

Okay, let's zero in on those *right* accounts. I personally have followed a course of never pursuing accounts that were smaller companies than mine. Ninety-nine percent of the time, they've given me more grief and aggravation because they either didn't understand the importance of good design, or they were undercapitalized.

What is the right account? First, it's an account your company wants and is suited to. You don't need to court accounts that only have one or two or three small jobs a year. Unless it's an annual report or corporate identity program, you don't need them. Remember it takes just as much time and energy to reel in a low roller as it does a high one. Make your moves count.

Let's further define what is the *right* account. It's a company or organization that is successful. 1) They are in a growth industry with a future. 2) They have a good credit rating. 3) They have a steady stream of work, and it's the kind that suits your design staff. 4) They understand or appreciate the need for good graphic design and its impact on their company's profitability.

Your company could unwittingly cause itself to look for the wrong accounts. Back in the 1980s, I watched many firms buy typesetting equipment. They thought that because they were spending a lot of money on type, they could pocket that money if they made typesetting an in-house service. I saw the writing on the wall, and because I could pass the costs on to my clients, I decided not to go into that business. It proved to be a smart move. The companies that did invest in typesetting wound up chasing customers for typesetting instead of design. That's because they had bought expensive equipment and hired typographers and proofreaders. Now they had to keep them busy when their designers weren't using them. This forced them toward the wrong accounts.

If your company is large, you may have a tough time trying to sell against freelance designers.

One design company even approached me to buy type from their typesetting division. Needless to say, I wasn't about to send work to a competitor. It would be bad enough for me to expose my accounts to them; I didn't need to fund them too. The reason I bring this up is to emphasize the importance of tailoring accounts to your company's strengths. Do not go off in a new direction unless the company is ready now. There are exceptions to this, such as multimedia, but don't leap into that technology until you've studied the market.

Who Is the Client?

Your clients have to feel they can trust your design firm completely. You have to treat them as if *they* are the client, not their company. After all, their necks are on the line. Many design companies in competition with yours have sales representatives who are savvy in the client/designer relationship. There are also firms that do not have anyone in sales and depend on the principal or principals to perform this function. This can be formidable competition if you're not a principal yourself.

Some clients may elect to work with one-person shops or freelancers. With the advent of the computer, there is an even larger cottage industry of these designers. Because they have less overhead, freelancers are generally cheaper than design companies. If your company is large, you may have a tough time selling against these designers. Work from your company's strengths. Go after accounts that need a full-service firm. These are usually large companies, not small businesses.

If your company is large, it has many pluses. There is back-up from the other designers in case of illness. A larger firm can usually live past thirty days if a client's policy is to pay in sixty. Larger firms can offer different types of talent to suit clients' projects. Larger design companies tend to attract talented designers because of their stability. There is also a consistency of quality when there is a staff to produce the work. Most large firms will never be too busy to take on more work.

...the bigger gun doesn't necessarily make the better marksman!

The principals of large firms are usually very savvy about print management, photo art direction, and the outsourcing of photography and illustration. And their reputations, if they are good, attract the best printing salespeople, photographers, and illustrators. Larger firms also keep extensive files on all of the current printing papers available, as well as examples of special effects.

Small firms/freelancers are usually less expensive. They often work out of their homes, where the rent for their business is nonexistent. Their equipment usually consists of a computer and some software programs. They may do excellent work, but service can slow dramatically if the designer is ill, has a family emergency, or has some other personal problem. If you are one of these free-lancers, try to have backup. Play on your strengths and go after accounts that fit your profile.

A note of warning. There are firms, as well as individuals, who are only selling technology. They may have all of the latest state-of-the-art computers. They may produce color separations in-house. But remember, you are selling design first. Computer design is two words, and only one of them is important. That word is "design," not "computer." Don't be surprised when some clients asks your company to give them roughs or thumbnails that aren't done on a computer. If this happens, I hope someone in your company can handle a marker.

Don't get trapped like the companies that flew into typeset-ting and ended up in Chapter Eleven. The company that approached me to buy typography from them is now out of busi-ness. This may be beyond your control, but hopefully you'll have some input with management. History has a funny way of repeat-ing itself if we don't profit from our mistakes. It's pretty dramatic that we've seen a whole industry like typography evaporate in five short years. People with decades of experience and incredible tal-ent have been erased by the computer.

CHAPTER 3

HOW TO NEVER HAVE TO COLD-CALL

Cold-calling is the most hated, feared, and emotionally debilitating part of sales. Many great designers can't cold-call, and yet they'll force themselves to do it. They may overcome their fear or intensify it.

The first step to selling graphic design is to realize that design is not fun and games. It's not the unnecessary embellishment of a printed piece, a package, or any other visual vehicle. Once you are convinced of this, you'll be more sure of what you are selling.

As I mentioned earlier, graphic design has earned great respect from the corporate heavyweights. They know the power of effective graphics. Why else would they have comprehensive graphic standards manuals to strictly govern the correct use of their corporate graphics? It's not ego. Companies do not throw money around without paybacks. This applies to their identities as well.

With every client on a tight budget, your company has to be creative in stretching their design dollar. There are many award-winning designs created in one or two colors that are just as compelling as designs in full color. You can make your client look good when they offer your savvy advice to their managers. And remember, when they look good, you look good.

The draft below is an example of a letter you can compose for someone referring *you to a prospect. You can make it as formal or informal as need be.*

S O U T H W E S T   P R I N T I N G ,   I N C .

100 Meridian Ave.
Washington, DC
20000

Phn (202) 555 1000 Fax (202) 555 2000

August 7, 1999

Ms. Jean Smith
Director of Corporate Relations
XYZ-Corporation
Z Street NW
Washington, DC 20000

Dear Jean,

I understand the XYZ Corporation is always interested in new sources for high-caliber graphic design projects. I recently met John Doe who is with Design+Associates, an award-winning, fifteen-year-old firm.

Design+Associates, Inc. (DAI) offers a unique blend of corporate and marketing design services that appear to fit your company's growth and goals. I feel they have a unique understanding of your industry, as well as the latest design technologies.

You probably hate receiving "cold-calls" as much as we all hate making them. John Doe will call you next week to see if he can take ten minutes of your time to introduce you to his company's work. If you feel this is inappropriate, please give me a call.

I hope your summer has gone well. I look forward to getting together with you in the near future.

Sincerely,

Joe Simpson

Joe Simpson
Vice President, Sales

The letter below is your own letter of introduction. To target this letter for its maximum effect, you'll need to do the homework I mentioned earlier.

1000 J Street NW
Suit 100
Washington, DC
10000

Phn (202) 555 1212
Fax (202) 555 1212

Design+Associates, Inc.

August 7, 1999

Ms. Jean Smith
Director of Corporate Relations
XYZ-Corporation
Z Street NW
Washington, DC 20000

Dear Ms. Smith,

Please let this letter serve as my introduction. I spoke with Mr. (Assistant) and I understand the XYZ Corporation is a leading force in the manufacturing of high-tech Widgets for the aerospace industry.

Design+Associates, Inc. (DAI) offers a distinctive blend of corporate and marketing design services that appear to fit your company's growth and goals. I would welcome the opportunity to share with you DAI's unique understanding of your industry and the latest design technologies.

You probably hate receiving "cold-calls" as much as I hate making them. I will call you next week to see if I can take ten minutes of your time to introduce you to our work.

Thank you for giving me the opportunity to introduce myself to you in writing.

Sincerely,

Jon Doe

Jonathan Doe
Account Executive

If you understand the prospective client's needs, you are way ahead of your competitors. Before your first verbal contact with prospects, do some research and find out as much as possible about them. If they are a Fortune 500 company, you know they produce an annual report. Get a copy of it and read it.

If they are primarily into marketing, you should focus on that aspect. There is no point in loading your portfolio full of annual reports if they are primarily producing direct mail pieces.

The Introduction

After reviewing everything you can find on your prospect, write a good, coherent letter of introduction. The letter should say how you were referred to this client. But beware, the person who gave you this lead may *not* be in good favor with your prospect. If possible, try to contact assistants who can answer some questions. Usually they will open up because they are keeping you from bothering their boss. Once they realize that you really want them, you're no longer a threat. Ask questions that are important:

1. What type of creative work is done in their department? See if you can pick up some samples.

2. What is the correct spelling of their boss's name and his or her title? One slip in spelling can mean disaster.

3. Are they happy with their designer/designers? They may say "yes" because the designer is a friend of theirs. But if they say "no," you've pressed the right button.

4. Does this person know the person who referred you to this account in the first place? If yes, press for a little more detail. You need to know if this is a plus or minus.

5. How are design decisions made? Is it usually through a committee? By now you may have worn out your welcome. If so, quit here.

Analyze the information you've received. Make an outline of the answers to your questions. That becomes the company story from start to end. The next step is to write and send your letter of introduction.

I once heard a house painter say that 90 percent of his job was preparation and only 10 percent was painting. Selling is a lot like that.

The Call

Before you make your formal call to the prospect, call the assistant to see if your letter arrived. Preparation is everything. I once heard a house painter say that 90 percent of his job was preparation and only 10 percent was painting. Selling is a lot like that.

The Interview

You've made the phone call, and if you're lucky, you've made an appointment with the key person. Prepare your portfolio carefully. Make notes as to which pieces relate to your prospect's needs. Also, realize that you are selling potential design, not what your company has already done. If need be, take less, but more tantalizing, work. And don't take a great printed sample if it has no relationship to your prospect's work. The exception is something like a coffee table book or something so special that it is a feather in your cap to have designed it.

Your company's portfolio is your most current sales tool. Always stack it for maximum effect. This means put the best work in the front. You should be able to tell when you've made your point and your prospect has seen enough. Don't overstay your welcome. I've seen salespeople ruin a call by not knowing when it was over. This also goes for closing a sale. Stop when you're ahead.

During the interview, it is helpful to ask procedural questions. How do they like layouts presented? Would they like to see them on the computer screen in your offices? You can explain that this is a way they can make minor changes before color proofs are pulled. Also ask how many concepts they normally like to see.

Overtime is a big consideration. Many firms pay their designers straight time for every hour they work. Others pay comp time, which is time off for overtime hours, and some companies expect salaried designers to work as long as it takes with no extra compensation. If your company does not charge a premium for overtime, you can use this to your advantage.

Turnaround/scheduling is important. You need to know what they consider normal turnaround for their kind of work. Most companies are used to quick turnarounds.

Invite them to your studio so they can meet the designers and see the facilities. This is a great way of reinforcing your credibility, but only if your company's offices are impressive. A lot of companies have nice offices, but only use freelancers when they have the work. If that's the case, you may have an empty office during a lull. I've heard studio owners say that they've brought people in off the street and paid them to look like they belonged there. I think this could be dangerous if the prospective client got into a conversation with the phony designer.

Show and Tell

One way to get a potential client to your offices is to develop an educational presentation for his or her staff. This could be a seminar on the stages involved in the design and production of an annual report or magazine. You can also suggest to your client that the seminar could help his or her staff understand the design and printing processes.

There are videos from manufacturers on the latest hardware and software. You can mix these into your presentation to give it some flash. Another angle is to invite a representative from a printing company that your company uses to be part of the presentation. They'll jump at the opportunity. This is also true of paper merchants and service bureau salespeople.

I would tell prospective clients that we hold seminars every Thursday from 10 A.M. to 12 noon. If I can accommodate more than one group, I'll include a printer, etc. If not, there's nothing wrong with a little one-on-one.

If your offices are inviting and in a convenient location for your client, you might offer a cost-break for holding meetings in your office for initial project consultation and layout presentation. After all, time is money.

I've often gotten clients to agree to meet in my offices by stressing the fact that I can pull samples of work we have previously done for other clients that might be applicable to their project. I have also used the excuse that I could have the art director and/or the designer present if the meeting were held in my office. Usually this works and valuable travel time is saved. Unless your clients are doctors or lawyers, they probably think their time is free when compared to your company's.

CHAPTER 4

POSITIONING YOUR COMPANY FOR MAXIMUM SALES

Today within the industry in general there are several dynamics working at the same time. There is a revolution of biblical proportions occurring in technology that everyone seems to be embracing. Everyone wants to look like they are in the know, but there is so much to learn that no one can grasp it all. Even the gurus have missed some of the basic rules of human relationships. There is also a common fear of the new technology that no one will talk about. As with the typesetting and printing industries, we are terrified of being replaced by computers. And in many cases justifiably so. You can take advantage of the confusion if you do your homework.

How Do You Position Your Company?

You and your company are in the consulting business. A lot of graphic design companies are trying to be something they're not. They want to be marketing firms, ad agencies, or some confused combination of all three. This again is the age of the specialist, and it applies to every industry. There's just too much for all of us to learn. Know your company's strengths and market them. Not what you wish were the strong points, but what's real.

I attended an Art Directors Club meeting some years ago. There were several firms that were doing government work consisting of "down-and-dirty" charts and graphs. The government was talking about giving all of their design work to one or two companies on a yearly contract. These companies would have to be very large because they were expected to also handle other services such as janitorial and furniture procurement. Needless to say, this would kill the small design firms that lived off of piecework from the government.

The majority of the designers at this meeting didn't feel it was worth their time and energy to help the threatened firms. This turned into a nasty exchange. The smaller government-oriented design firms threatened to go after our private sector clients if we didn't help them fight for their business. They said they'd "eat our lunch." This was an idle threat because their companies operated in a different stratum from ours, but we realized the seriousness of their plight.

The moral of this story is: know your company's real strengths and concentrate on them. The firms I mentioned thought they could instantly enter the private sector and challenge firms specializing in graphics, even though the government-oriented firms had no experience in the private sector. That's not saying these companies aren't capable of better design and shouldn't go after better clients than they have at this time, but it's hard enough to sell what your company does well, let alone what it would like to do.

You Can Become Your Client's Best Ally

If you take the time to learn the new design technology, you will probably have done something most other design account executives haven't. Lunches are a great place to cultivate a trusting relationship. Your clients can ask questions without their peers being present. Don't take this lightly. A lot of people in sales think that misery loves company. With the new technology, this isn't true; nobody wants to appear to be a "techno-dummy" in front of co-workers or especially his or her boss. The business world is a jungle and everyone can use help in coping with the quickly changing design techology.

How You Can Save Your Client Real Money

As I said, the new technology can in fact be your greatest ally. You can show your client the true cost savings as well as time savings. Once again, remember that all services that someone else buys for clients are going to be marked up. Even if the purchaser tells them otherwise, they're going to pay somewhere. No one can stay in business giving away services, and brokering is a service.

The Art of Anti-Brokering

I may be considered a heretic by many in the graphic design business when I explain my philosophy for handling outside services such as prepress and printing. I am not a broker, nor do I want to be. That means I do not buy and sell those services. I have them billed directly to my client, and I bill my client a management fee or 10 percent of the printer's invoice. That fee is less than the standard 15 or 20 percent markup. If your company wants to buy those services and mark them up, then stop reading until the next chapter.

First, explain your company's business philosophy to your clients. Now offer to put them in contact with a good service bureau (usually, a former typographer). Explain that the bureau can supply high resolution paper or film output. (On the other hand, if you place ads for them, you can buy the negatives. This is a minor expense compared to the film output for a large brochure or magazine. You can handle this, and you will have more control with your own service bureau.)

If your client is in charge of a publication, they can furnish their printer with film. Make sure they get a printing quote *with* and *without* film so they can compare costs. If they are not comfortable with this, you can offer to have the film prepared and just have the service bureau bill them.

Explain to them that they can also save money by using one of the many printers who are now entering the electronic prepress arena with in-house service. However, it makes more sense for them to buy their own film if their printer does not have an *in-house* capability of generating the negatives electronically.

Some printers will say they have the ability to take electronic files. This doesn't mean they are not farming out their prepress services. As their consultant, recommend that your client ask those printers, point-blank, if their prepress is done totally in-house. Tell them not to be timid. It's a justifiable concern and deserves a direct response.

If your prospective client's company hasn't made the shift to using disks for copy, encourage them to do it now. Most design and printing companies are working with IBM WordPerfect or Microsoft Word disks. And make sure they don't use double-density disks, which are only good on IBM compatible systems. Ask them to go through their company and confiscate them, and then make sure everyone has a supply of high-density disks.

With Macintosh Power PCs, the IBM connection has become even easier for all of us.

Let Them Know You're a Free Consultant

Your prospective client's biggest ally will be you. They should use you as a consultant and call you if there is a procedure they're not sure of. Remember, they know you won't laugh at a question, and they know you're not in a position to use their lack of knowledge to make them look bad in your company. There are some people who, when lost in a new city, will never ask for directions. Just think, if their time is worth money, how stupid this would be. And your client's time is worth money.

I have watched savvy clients guess about the answers to questions a designer could have answered instantly. This may be human nature, but it doesn't have to be your clients' approach. They'll look good when they seem to have solved a technical problem all by themselves. When you become part of your clients' arsenal of protection, you'll be an asset they won't want to lose.

You want your clients to remember you for what you did say,

not what you didn't. No one likes surprises in business, because they are rarely good ones.

Beware of Competitive Computer Gurus

There are designers and professional consultants who are ready at a moment's notice to tell your client about their insights into electronic design and prepress technology, while trying to make your client believe they know more than you do.

Beware! I have heard some really off-the-wall observations from these so-called consultants. These people believe only what they have been exposed to and have a closed mind to other areas of technology. Often a salesman of computer hardware or software has convinced your so-called guru competitor that their hardware or software is the best, and now it's gospel. No one needs this kind of advice.

Your client needs to get answers because money is at stake. Call some experienced peers. These people, like you, depend on the right answers. We will get into networking later in this book, but right now meet others whose responsibilities in their companies are similar to yours. You probably get two or three invitations a week to trade shows, lectures, industry seminars, and conferences. Take advantage of them.

CHAPTER 5

PROMOTING YOUR COMPANY

Promotion is an art form and many fine books have been written on the subject. Whether you work for a large company or a small firm, promotion can help it survive. Here I'll use my own experience to highlight some of the basics that will work for any graphic design company.

My lawyer once invited me to a partners' dinner meeting to discuss his firm's new marketing approach. He explained that this was a monthly meeting of the partners to plan strategies. I thought that I would be part of a discussion on how to market the law firm to the public.

Wrong! After dinner I was introduced as the person who would now give the partners a seminar on the new marketing plan for their firm. This caught me by surprise, to say the least. Not wanting to embarrass my host, I decided to wing it. Fortunately I knew the basics and, most of all, used common sense. Marketing, after all, is not a mystery.

First I told the partners that it was their individual responsibility to sell for the firm, not by cold-calling, but by joining the Rotary Club, the Chamber of Commerce, or other community organizations. Next they needed a P.R. plan. This meant that someone had to be in charge of sending out press releases whenever something newsworthy happened in the firm.

I told them that they also needed a simple brochure that was nothing more than an extension of their business card. This brochure would fit in a standard business envelope, and each partner's bio would be on a single sheet in a pocket in the back of the brochure.

I then talked about a simple but catchy series of ads. These ads would be very general, simply promoting the law firm as a reputable and multitalented group of partners versus a group of ambulance chasers.

Everything I said was based on common sense. These ideas weren't new, except for the ad concepts.

Last but not least, I remembered a large clock on their reception area wall. I couldn't resist an experiment. I told the lawyers that any of them could run a little late for a client's appointment, some more than others. The clock was an unnecessary reminder to those waiting in the reception area, of just how late they were running. After all, it takes a conscious effort to look at a watch versus just looking up from a magazine at a wall clock.

I was given a hearty round of applause for my little common sense approach to marketing. Two weeks later, I was in my lawyer's office reception area. There was a big pale spot on the wall above the receptionist. I asked, "What happened to the clock?"

She replied, "I'm not really sure. About two weeks ago the partners came in one morning and the next thing I knew, the clock was gone."

I smiled to myself.

Marketing is a Necessity

Marketing is a series of necessary efforts to promote your company. The only difference between your company and a law firm is your imagination or knowledge. Don't bite off more than you can chew, but don't be so sure you can't bite off quite a bit. Be aware that you are marketing your company in any business situation.

Remember the lawyers? Hoping for another solution, I asked a person in my firm what they would've done if asked to come up with an instant marketing seminar. I got a blunt answer, "I would've thrown up!"

Marketing is only effective when it's used. I've been to many good seminars on the "how to" of marketing and have seen people forget everything they paid money to learn as soon as they got back to their office. No game plan will guarantee no results. Marketing is work, but you can see results.

I also like to remind the principals of design firms and other businesses that, when times are tough, they should not forget that they were the reason for the company's original success. They should remain active in the day-to-day sales efforts of the business.

Let's Look at You and Your Company

Some design companies already have a public relations program in place. Look around at yours. Don't be too quick to offer suggestions until you thoroughly understand what has been done in the past and have decided what you want to do now. I have seen many a shot from the hip come back as a ricochet to the heart, and this can be a killer for future projects.

Usually a public relations program has an author. Find out if that author is still around. You don't need surprises. Suppose that person is now above you. That person may also be able to tell you if the campaign was effective and why.

First, Clean House

The best way to get your company's P.R. juices flowing is to hold an open house. This is a great way to promote your company and to get the facilities cleaned up. I've even used this as a deadline to have a corporate brochure printed. This is a method used in business everyday. If there is no tangible deadline, it's not unusual for there to be no tangible product. It's also imperative for top management to understand and back this concept.

Don't take the open house lightly. There should be a theme. I know of one firm that holds a Valentine's Day party for their clients. After all, February is a partyless month. You can usually negotiate a good deal with a caterer. You can use the open house to announce a new product or service, a company anniversary, or any other excuse to invite clients to your offices.

Corporate Brochure

Every design company needs a brochure. Business people used to exchange business cards whenever they would meet. Now a company brochure is considered the best way to introduce yourself to the world. Your company brochure doesn't have to be fancy. It doesn't have to be expensive. But it had better be good. In this age of information, people are inundated with good graphics and good brochures. The difference between conservative and mundane is a fine line. Often good design is the best differential for making your message stand out in the crowd.

Obviously if you are seeking high level clients you will need a brochure that addresses a much higher level of design. I once heard a designer say that he didn't have a brochure because samples of his past work for clients took its place. If that's the case, make sure you have a lot of samples to leave behind.

Designers' Biographies

Update your designers' biographies and make them more exciting. I like to call these "profiles." You can really spice them up. Most people have very dull résumés because they are naturally embarrassed to toot their own horn too loudly. A profile is written about someone, not by them. There is no reason why someone's obituary should be more exciting than their biography was when they were alive.

Profiles are much simpler than biographies or résumés, which are usually dry and very unexciting. The profiles should be relatively short, but they should be just as meaty as the best résumé. If you are going to write the profiles, ask each designer for a current copy of his or her résumé. If it's really current, you may want to think about the designer's relationship with new accounts.

Most people have a hard time writing their own bio or profile. Their professional credentials take on a very matter-of-fact tone. It's not because they have poor credentials. On the contrary, they could be brilliant, but as I said earlier, it is always hard for people to step back and give themselves a glowing résumé.

There's an art to writing a good profile. For example, one of my employees had only a little professional experience prior to working for me. Her résumé was sparse. She was very timid when talking about herself, but she was quite the opposite when verbalizing her work.

There is no reason why someone's obituary should be more exciting than their biography was when they were alive.

I had to really work on her profile to give her credibility. And I couldn't lie. She was clearly someone who was very talented, despite her lack of experience. She was born in Europe and I decided to make this a big plus. I played on her strengths and the recent successes she had while working on projects in my studio. *It's a fact that a bad résumé may keep a wonderful prospective employee from ever being considered for a job.* Her resulting profile is shown on the next page.

Once you've learned to write an effective profile, you will be able to offer this service to your clients. Many companies include biographies in their corporate brochures. They also use them in proposals. The profile is also an awesome résumé.

Design+Associates, Inc.

Profile

Jane Smith

Senior Designer

Ms. Smith is a senior designer with Design+Associates. Whether she is directing a special project or participating as a key member of a design team, Ms. Smith offers an array of special talents. She is highly skilled in illustration and photography and has a thorough knowledge of the complex Macintosh programs that D+A utilizes.

Ms. Smith has worked with national accounts, bringing a unique European flair to everyday design problems. She is proficient in her knowledge of all aspects of the prepress process and has worked with the latest prepress technologies.

Prior to joining Design+Associates, Ms. Smith was a designer at Electric Images in New York. Before that, she freelanced for Studio XL in New Jersey and also freelanced for Jones, Hunt & Simms in Connecticut.

Ms. Smith graduated with honors and a BFA from The University of Buffalo, College of Art and Design. She also studied at the Swiss School of Design in Basel, Switzerland, as well as The University of Rome in Italy.

Ms. Smith is fluent in both French and Italian.

The All-Important Press Release

The press release is an excellent way to blow your company's horn. First collect the names and addresses of editors and publications in which you want to have your releases published. Always remember that a press release has to feature newsworthy information. It can announce a person's promotion or some new product breakthrough, but it can't sell. I can't emphasize this strongly enough.

The structure of a typical press release is an inverted triangle, with the bulk of information at the top and the least important at the bottom. This way the editor can chop it off at the end of any paragraph without losing vital information.

Press releases should be categorized by subject, and you can make up a file of specific publications and editors for each type of subject. For instance, trade journals will often publish employee promotions and new arrivals. Other publications will print stories on new accounts that you have landed. Look through magazines and trade tabloids to see which ones print what.

Editors are often looking for news. If you can get to know some of the key editors, it's not inappropriate to call them and sound them out on a potential release. If you're good at writing, you may be able to turn a press release into an article. A sample press release is shown on the next page.

A press release has to give the following information:

1. *Who* is the subject (if it's about a person).

2. *What* has happened that is newsworthy.

3. *When* did the event occur.

4. *Where* did the event occur.

5. *Why* is it newsworthy.

Last but not least, you should give your name and phone number for more information.

Press Release

Design+Associates Inc.

For Immediate Release:

Washington, D.C.–based Design+Associates announces a breakthrough in photo retouching. Their development of D+A Interactive Software offers an electronic retouching package equal to those of the large prepress systems costing hundreds of thousands more.

Design+Associates spokesman, John Smith, says the break-through will give small design studios the capability of competing with the large prepress labs.

The software uses a sophisticated paint system with a Macintosh 840 Quadra. The software cost is approximately $10,000 and a complete workstation is double that amount.

For further information contact Jane Doe at: (202) 555-5555.

Please note that the press release on the previous page comes dangerously close to selling and probably would only be picked up by trade publications.

I've found it very helpful to list publications, the names of their editors, and their addresses and to file them under specific areas of interest. My *List A* contains all of the publications. My *List B* contains high tech publications for product announcements. *List C* contains general interest publications for personnel announcements and other general company news. You can arrange your lists to suit your needs.

The Map

If your company is in a remote area, such as an industrial park, develop a postcard-sized map for prospective visitors. The map can be very simple, but clear. Everyone in the company should be encouraged to use it.

Advertising

If your company is large, it probably places advertising for its clients. (This is an area that's often overlooked by small companies.) Since advertising doesn't have a defined result, it is usually the last area to receive a defined budget. But advertising can work for your company just as it does for its clients.

If your company doesn't buy advertising, but it does have a budget, work up a game plan. Many small companies find it profitable to advertise in the yellow pages.

Some companies also spend time and money advertising in trade publications. Since these are read only by their competitors, this has never made much sense to me.

You can create simple ads. You can be the writer and place the ads yourself, remembering that the secret to successful advertising is frequency. It does no good to run an ad once and then pull it. The public is very busy, so you have to hit them over the head by running your ad numerous times to get their attention.

I've seen ads generate new business three months after the last one appeared in a publication. It's a lot like fishing. You have to be patient and hang in there. The more patience, the bigger the fish.

The Clock

Don't forget the clock in your company's reception area. Get rid of it now. This may have been a second thought in my marketing seminar, but it could make your visitors a lot happier and enhance your total promotional effort.

The Marketing Consultant

Marketing is a company effort. Everyone counts. If your ideas are falling on management's deaf ears, hire a marketing consultant. This is not because they know more than you do, but because someone outside the company usually lacks hidden agendas. It's true that management will often assign more worth to something they pay for. An example of this is a case close to home.

An outside voice is often listened to, because an insider must be part of the problem.

I asked an editor friend of mine, as a consultant, to read this book and to feel free to use her infamous red pen. She did, and my manuscript was a sea of red marks. I decided to make only limited changes. She had added numerous commas and I questioned almost all of them.

It was agreed upon by both of us up front that I would receive a bill for her services. When I got her bill a few days later, I looked at her work quite differently. I made every single correction that she had marked. After all, I paid for all of those commas.

It has often been said that an outside voice is listened to by management because an insider must be part of the problem. Whether it's true or not, it is a fact that can't be ignored. So go with the flow. Hire a consultant who shares your views.

Promoting Your Company on the Internet

The Internet is a relatively young arena for commerce. To understand how the Internet can be a viable marketing tool for your design firm, you must study how the Worldwide Web is being used successfully by your competition.

The Internet is not always a friendly place to be. A site that doesn't work, is too slow, or is just plain boring can be poison to the advertiser and the viewer. Think of Web pages as ads. Yes, full page, living color, real-time advertisements. The Internet is a giant catalog filled with valuable information as well as ads. Some of the ads are great and some are terrible, but they all have one thing in common, they are ads.

The Internet is like a giant television network running nothing but commercials. Would you tune into a station that just showed commercials? I know the only time I have made it a point to watch commercials was to view the art directors' club's winners for the funniest and most memorable spots produced during the year.

If your company is already designing Web pages, move onto the next section. If not, you need to learn as much about cyberspace as possible. Your clients will want to work with a design firm that can take care of all their design needs. For this reason, if no other, your company must have a Web page. Don't think that it will snag hot potential clients who are surfing the Internet just hoping to find a company like yours. You'll need a striking, vibrant page for those potential clients you meet and invite to see your company's portfolio electronically.

If you don't have the technical people in your company to produce a page, remember, you do have the designers who can best show off your firm's work. You can align your group with savvy Web consultants and programmers who can follow your designers' art direction and layouts, and create a great page.

The fact that your company has a Web page should not lead you to sell pages to clients unless you have a team ready to produce top notch sites. If your company is just starting out in cyberspace, you'll be competing with other design firms that are way ahead of yours and this could become embarrassing.

Take advantage of seminars and conferences on the art of designing and marketing on the Internet.

What If There's No Budget for Marketing

If this is the case in your company, you'll have to get creative. Clip competitor's advertisements. Go to design trade shows and pick up competitors' brochures as well as other handouts. If your company's materials need to be redesigned, collect good examples of competitors' promos, stationery, and logos. I suggest mounting the examples on presentation boards. If your company has access to the Internet, but doesn't have a site, find some good home pages developed by and for design firms. These can be downloaded in color or shown on a monitor.

Now it's time to sit down with management. Show them what the competition is doing, and discuss ways of moving funds from one budget to another. Namely, to yours. Read as many books on marketing as you can find. The public library is a good source.

There are things that don't require much money. The press releases and the designers' biographies require little. You may want to hire a professional writer but, in the case of the bios, it will be a one-time expense. The map can be one color and inexpensive to print, but I would suggest that you have one of your company's graphic designers make it simple and attractive.

An Internet presence is more expensive, but it may be absolutely necessary for you to compete in your marketplace.

CHAPTER 6

NETWORKING EFFECTIVELY

Networking is very important in any sales position. But a lot of people make the mistake of thinking they should network with their peers. Wrong! Your peers are not going to give you any business, and they certainly won't refer you to clients. Of course there is an exception to that rule. If your company is outrageously expensive, your competitors will offer up your name when they are asked by a new client to give them other names for a bid.

Research Your Potential Clients' Clubs or Groups

There are many different types of groups that can generate business. As I mentioned in the previous chapter concerning the lawyers, you can join community organizations like the Jaycees, Rotary, and Kiwanis Clubs. These groups perform community services, and they can always use the talent of a design company. This is not to say your company will be doing a ton of free work. The other members of these groups are professionals and realize the time you give is valuable.

If you join a group, plan to get involved. You will be visible if you get on some key committees. There are people who join a group and expect networking without any personal investment. They'll meet a few people, but they'll never be as effective as you.

I joined the Jaycees twenty years ago. My old friends are now the presidents of companies. This has helped me throughout my career and it really helps now. Even if you're in a rural area, there will be some sort of group that you can join. Most small towns have a Lions Club.

Professional Organizations are Important

I'm not saying you shouldn't belong to organizations relating to the field of graphic design. The art directors' clubs are great places to learn what's going on in the field. They offer technical forums as well as social events. And let's face it, you might meet your next employer at one of these meetings.

... you might meet your next employer at one of these meetings.

The American Institute of Graphic Arts (AIGA) is expensive to join, but worth the dues. Their publications, shows, and conferences are first rate. If you are from a graphic design background, you already know this. But if you're not, you will need to learn everything you can about the field. You need to know as much as the designers, if you are going to represent them in the marketplace. That doesn't mean you have to be a designer.

I've included a list of national graphic design and other related organizations as well as publications in this chapter. Staying on top of what is going on is a form of networking. I have also listed several relevant community organizations. The new Graphic Communications Association, formerly Printing Industries of America, has chapters in many states. This is an excellent organization for networking with printers. I've received many leads from printing salespeople. They have their ear to the ground and can become clients themselves. They will often have more of an inside track than you do. And don't forget the paper promotion people that visit your company with samples of the latest papers.

Since most clients come through referrals, you need exposure. You need to do some research on what organizations your potential clients will join. For instance, if you want to do annual reports, there are groups of financial analysts who meet and would welcome a presentation on the design process for producing an annual report.

There are organizations you can join that will not only expose you to potential clients, but also expand your knowledge and give you leadership skills. Remember, you only get out of an organization what you put into it. The people who are visible are the doers, not the silent observers.

I have listed the national offices of organizations worth investigating. These are too important to bury in the appendix of this book. You can find out if they have a local group in your area and pursue it if you're interested in it.

Graphic Communications Association (GCA)
100 Dangerfield Road
Alexandria, VA 22314-2888

(703) 519-8160

GCA used to be the Printing Industries of America and has chapters in cities all over the country.

International Association of Business Communicators (IABC)
One Hallidie Plaza
Suite 600
San Francisco, CA 94102

(415) 433-3400

IABC is involved with the issues of business communications. They hold local and national conferences and seminars.

Jaycees
1258 N. Highland, #209
Los Angeles, CA

(213) 465-8707

The Jaycees used to be the Junior Chamber of Commerce. If you're under thirty, this is a great place to build lasting professional and personal relationships.

The Rotary
250 Park Avenue South
New York, NY 10003

(212) 674-0500

The Rotary clubs are community oriented and will give you an entree to many business and civic leaders.

The U.S. Chamber of Commerce
11 West 20 Street
New York, NY 10011

(212) 463-7730

Each city usually has a Chamber of Commerce. This is an excellent area for meeting the community's movers and shakers.

Selling is best done when you are not aware that you are selling. Interpersonal relationships need to develop to form lasting bonds that will keep clients from jumping ship. You need to be a problem-solver as well as a mentor. Remember what we learned earlier: The client is the *person,* not the company he or she works for. This is where business friendship becomes so important.

Just as with any successful relationship, you must work at nurturing your business friendships. A part-time effort will yield nothing. Your client has a full-time job, and he or she expects the same from you.

Success Breeds Success

Failure breeds contempt. No matter how bad things get, you must draw on your past successes. Everyone has a little bad luck. If you hit a streak of lost sales or accounts that don't pan out, only your mind can make this a big or small setback.

Don't take business personally. People are attracted to different design firms for myriad reasons. Designers are very sensitive, or they wouldn't have the temperament necessary to be great. You have to be the proverbial cheerleader. If you're down, it will show to your co-workers. Since you're the point-person, this can have a devastating effect.

CHAPTER 7

Selling Good Design to Clients with Low Budgets

As mentioned earlier, graphic design is not fun and games to the prospective client. It's not the unnecessary embellishment of a printed piece, a package, or any other visual vehicle. I've noticed that companies who are the most competitive and fighting for their place in their market seem to be fully aware of the cost and effect relationship of their marketing dollars. They can't afford to shotgun, they must take careful aim at their targets, or customers.

There is good, mediocre, and bad graphic design. What your clients get depends on your company's knowledge and judgement, not their budget. Budgets only restrict how much money they can spend, not how much design they can get. If they spend money wisely, they're corporate heros. But a poor end-product will also be remembered, not how much they saved their company in design dollars.

If your clients are using IBM equipment for word processing, you should ask which software they use. The most prevalent programs are WordPerfect and Microsoft Word. PageMaker is used by some companies, but not the majority. QuarkXPress is the most popular page make-up software and, at this time, the most prepress-friendly of any of the page layout software programs. There are some companies that have bought PageMaker and feel it's best. Each software program is constantly improving.

During the interview you should say who will be working on the prospect's projects. It is best for the client to meet with the actual designer. No one needs layers of bureaucracy to get in the way of a time-sensitive project.

Turnaround/scheduling is important. If clients ask, you should know what the normal turnaround is for their kind of work. Most designers and design firms are used to quick turnaround, and you may elect to go into this at the time you are awarded a real project. After I've gotten to know clients, I tell them that it's wise to try to keep schedules reasonable, so that when the real crunch comes, the designers know it's not just another false-alarm.

Budgets only restrict how much money your clients can spend, not how much design they can get.

I once had a client who said every job was rush. My reply was, if every job was rush, then what job was really rush? That client finally saw the light and did become more judicious with his deadlines. Common sense says that there must be an order to priorities.

Getting the Most for the Least

Now it's time to look at how prospective clients can get the most for their design dollar. First they need to know what their budget is. Then they should share it with you. You can't work blind and still offer effective solutions.

They should have rough copy or final copy if it is available. They should bring all photos, logos, or other existing artwork that has to be incorporated into the piece. Quantity (number of printed copies) will tell you many things. It will let you know whether foil stamping, die-cutting, or embossing are practical. Quantity will also have a budget-bearing effect on the number of colors, varnishes, and other printing matters. It will often have a bearing on the grade of paper selected.

As a rule, small quantities are fine for special effects like stamping or embossing, and the best grades of papers can be used without significant cost increase within your printing budget. Long press runs make special effects expensive, and the grade of paper a significant cost factor. If you're not sure of what is practical, call your printer. Provide a rough schedule or final schedule with key dates.

The Limited Use of Color Can Still Be Effective

There are other ways to get more out of your client's graphic design dollar. You can offer a three-color effect from over-printing two colors. This should be easy for your designers. You can also achieve classic designs with the use of just black and white.

Have some pieces in your portfolio showing examples of this. It is an art not every designer can pull off. Hopefully yours can. If you use only one color, it does not have to be black. There are dark PMS colors that look black until they are screened back. Also, there are colored papers that offer a second color look when combined with the right inks.

Some of the best design I've ever seen was done in black and white. This was when the lack of color became a powerful statement of simplicity. Newspaper design has always utilized the power of black ink to make strong design statements.

Tricks of the Trade

What if your client has no photographs available and can't afford stock photography or illustration? A good designer can work award-winning wonders with typography alone. Charts and graphs can become illustrations. *Fortune* magazine did this in the fifties and sixties. The real restriction on your clients' projects isn't money, it's imagination. It's your design company's imagination that will make the difference.

Tell clients not to be afraid to rough out what they want. Designers welcome the client's organization of the key elements. This tells the designer what the client feels is important. It will not restrict them. They will use the sketch as a point of departure.

The most compelling image on a printed piece is the human figure or face.

It is another thing for the client to add elements after a design is complete. Think of it this way. You design a beautiful living room in your house. Each piece of furniture is carefully placed in a spot that maximizes its beauty and function. Suddenly someone shows up with a baby grand piano and insists you make room for it. You can't just move some things around without destroying the design of the room. The piano is now the dominant element and the other furniture must work around it. You have to rethink the whole design because the piano is the focal point.

It has been said that the most compelling image you can use on a printed piece is the human figure or face. To prove this, visit a newsstand. When you are standing in front of it, turn your back on the publications. Now turn around. The publications that feature people on the covers will draw your eye to them much faster than the ones with cars, motorcycles, or boats. Designers have always known this, and they use this effectively on everything from annual reports to point-of-sale posters.

Coping with limited budgets can make you an asset in the client's eyes. Use it to your advantage. Creativity is the most important part of budget-restricted projects. The client can cut back on many things such as paper, number of colors, or quantity printed, but not good design.

You're a Diplomat

If you are representing designers, you must be a diplomat with them as well as your client. If the budget is on the low side, you must make sure your client won't get an inferior job. The designer must be made aware that each project is an investment in solidifying an account. But if despite all of this the client's budgets are too low, look for another client. If this project is the exception to the rule, make it known to the art director or the designer (depending on how your studio works). If you contemplate difficulties with the design staff over budget, ask management to intercede and explain the situation to the designer or art director.

Remember, it's up to management to make sure your jobs run through the studio smoothly.

CHAPTER 8

WRITING YOUR WINNING PROPOSAL

The most important factor in the success of a design project is the bid process. The expression "apples and oranges" is quite appropriate. If several design companies are bidding on a project, it is very important that each bids on the same requirements or specifications. Good written information is an absolute necessity, and a meeting with all parties at the same time is the optimum. Many companies simply send out a Request for Proposal (RFP). Another name for this is a Request for Quotation (RFQ). The U.S. Government has a better system. They hold formal bid conferences and they bid out everything.

The Bid Conference

If your client is not holding bid conferences on complex projects, you should suggest that they will reap some benefits from such conferences, and that they're actually doing themselves a disservice by not holding them. Explain that when all of the design companies or representatives are present at once, they can ask questions, and each will hear the same answers. If one design company receives an RFP in the mail or in an individual meeting, that design company may have a legitimate question or, even better, a more economical suggestion for producing the job. If the idea has merit and changes the scope of the work, the client should notify the other designers individually of the new specifications.

On the other hand, the bid conference can be a hotbed of good ideas, if the client lets the participants feel they are shaping the project for the better. This is fact. I've seen it happen over and over again.

There is another apple-and-orange factor to be considered. The design firms for the project should be approximately the same type and size. Except for small projects that usually don't warrant a full-fledged bid conference, the types of firms or individual designers should be of equal talent and capability. If the client elects to use either freelancers or large design firms, it is better that they are similar to each other. They wouldn't invite a large printer and a quick-print shop to the same bid conference for a printing project. The same holds true with design firms.

Be Thorough: Read the RFP

I've found the greatest mistake most clients make when writing specifications is not being clear. They often use a businesslike tone but forget to include key information. You need to read the RFP carefully and quickly so you can ask questions immediately.

For instance, I recently received an RFP for a complex project that involved the design and production of a brochure. The client was very explicit about the quality expected, the deadline, the number of colors, and the dimensions. But the information on the number of pages was missing. When I asked about the page count, I was told there would be between twenty and thirty. My client was very busy and didn't want to get into a discussion about the project. This told me that I would have to fill in some holes.

Since the specifications told me the project was a saddle-stitched brochure, I knew the number of pages had to be divisible by four. (Four pages equal one sheet bound in a saddle-stitched brochure, as you can see if you pull the staples out of a *Time* magazine.) Also, the most economical way to run this job is in multiples of eights or sixteens. Neither was an option without a discussion with the client. So, to solve the dilemma and make sure I would be covered, I simply gave a per-page price. I don't know what my competition did. I do know the client was going to be even busier later trying to get comparative bids.

A proposal can be as simple or as complex as you want it to be. Let's look at the most complex, because, after that, you can decide what you want to omit. There are usually four parts to a bid. The first is your design firm's *Capabilities Statement.* The second is the *Project Overview.* The third is the *Technical Proposal* and the fourth is a *Cost Proposal.* Each of the four is often said to carry equal weight. Cost is a consideration when each firm has met the other criteria.

I have also seen some companies ask for a layout with the proposal. This is against the American Institute of Graphic Arts and Graphic Artists Guild's Codes of Ethics, and it is also against the Graphic Design Trade Customs (reviewed later in this book). This issue is currently under review by the FTC. It has been determined by the United States Justice Department that no one can stop a designer from doing "spec work," as this, they feel, causes the restriction of competition. But I feel the majority of designers in the industry believe that it's unethical to ask for such services.

Design firms, unlike advertising agencies, are not counting on millions of dollars in ad revenues to enable them to offer free or speculative work. They bill by the hour for services rendered. Spec work is free work, and it's usually worth what prospective clients pay for it.

Some clients who wish to see multiple concepts will offer each firm an equal fee to come up with a design concept. If the fee is just a token, they may get three inferior designs and thus an inferior final product. This is often a waste of money because the client picks one of the firms and makes them start the design process all over again.

After a thorough portfolio review with each participating design firm and the submission of a detailed proposal, a client should have enough input to make an intelligent decision.

Responding to a Request for Proposal (RFP)

The Letter: A letter introducing you and your company is the formal way to preface your bid on a project. The letter should give a very brief overview of the project from your standpoint. Be sure to describe the level of quality you intend to offer. The letter can be informal or formal, but don't make the mistake of putting some key observations in it and leaving them out of the proposal. Since the letter is usually to an individual, his or her peers may not see it. If the proposal has to go through a committee, it can become separated from the proposal and will not be a part of the decision process.

It's to your advantage to make the proposal as clear as possible. You won't get a phone call from the client because of unclear prose. You won't get the project either. They may think you don't know your job, and this sign of weakness could come back to haunt you later.

1. Capabilities Statement: This is the area within the proposal to show why your company is the best suited for this project. It can contain a history of the firm, as well as past experience your company has had in managing similar projects.

2. Project Overview: This part of the proposal contains several key elements that explain to the client what you perceive the scope of work to be, as well as what they will provide. Don't just parrot back their specifications. Show some thinking on your part.

A. Background. This is your interpretation of the history of the piece to be designed, if it has one. Also, you can describe the goals/purpose of the project. This overview is important in showing your understanding of how their company does business.

B. Work Requirement. This is a complete description of the project's specifications, such as: size, number of pages, number of colors, photographic or illustration treatments, methods of presentation of layouts, types of page proofs, how the copy will be presented (on disk or manuscript), and the number of copies to be printed. This is the "meat and potatoes" of the project. Any special effects you may want to use can be highlighted in this section.

3. Technical Proposal: The technical proposal is a description of the scope of work from your point of view, as well as your insights as to how the project's production process can be improved. This is not a verbal description of design solutions, nor a free design consultation. It is meant to show the client that the designer isn't going to approach their project with a cookie-cutter or standardized method. They are paying for a custom job, and they will accept no less.

4. Cost Proposal: The cost proposal should contain only the cost of work and expenses spelled out in the client's "Statement of Work and Requirements." Author's alterations, unless you know exactly what they will be and can convey this to the client, should not be included in the proposal. Other unknown out-of-pocket expenses must also be excluded. Hourly rates can be assigned by you for services that may be needed, such as print management, photo art direction, illustration, preparation of charts and graphs, copywriting, keyboarding of text, and anything else that might be part of the scope of work but has not yet been defined. Most companies use cost as a parameter, not as a specific criteria, in evaluating the proposal.

As I mentioned earlier, it's important to spell out in the proposal exactly what you are furnishing. I once submitted a proposal to design a logo for a company. After submitting three rounds of concepts that seemed to be going nowhere, I called the president of the company and explained that I would need more money to continue. His statement to me was: "The quote was for the design of a logo, and you haven't designed one yet." You can bet that will never happen to me again. I specify exactly how many concepts the client will get for the quote.

This may seem like common sense, but often we don't see a bad client coming. In sales, we usually assume that everyone is as honest as we are. And it's probably the only way to stay optimistic.

Other Elements

Each proposal will be judged in its entirety. The client may not have asked for the following but you may wish to consider these elements anyway.

A. Time-line Management. This is the specific time-line for completing the project.

B. Project Staff Profiles. These are the biographies of the staff who will be assigned to this project.

C. Client List. A list of your design firm's clients similar to the company requesting the proposal.

D. Graphic Design Trade Customs. These are the terms your company uses to conduct business. It is very important that they be shown to a prospective client prior to beginning any work. Your company can use any part or all of the customs.

It's important to spell out exactly what you are furnishing in the proposal.

The Question Never Asked

Let's say the proposal you're working on is a yearly project. Most salespeople are timid when it comes to the crucial question that begs to be asked. The question is: "What did you pay for this job last year?" The client doesn't have to tell you, but very often they will. The meek may inherit the earth, but they probably won't get this project. Sometimes clients will think it's not kosher to give out that information.

There's a rationale that they can't argue with. If they tell what they spent before, there's a good chance the bid or bids will come in lower than the previous year.

If the project is new, ask them if they have a budget in mind. They will often include printing with the total budget. If so, you can get a rough printing estimate and subtract that amount.

The Exit

If you don't get the project, don't stop there. Call the client and request a critique of your proposal. Also, don't burn a bridge. Write a letter telling the client that your company is available if things don't work out with your competitor. This will be appreciated and you may get another chance. Jobs can make enemies out of clients and designers almost as easily as they can make friends.

CLOSING THE DEAL

*The fine art of selling is knowing how to
close the deal.*

CHAPTER 9

SELLING GRAPHIC DESIGN VERSUS DESKTOP DESIGN

To sell graphic design, you must be selling design, not desktop design. If you represent a company that specializes in production and not design, this chapter will help you understand the difference. There's no reason why you can't still be an effective salesperson, you just need to know your niche and stay in an environment that is compatible with your company's type of work.

Desktop Design

Desktop design is the laying out of images on a page. To a desktop designer, the blank page is the equivalent of a grand puzzle. The text, illustrations, charts, and photographs are all pieces of the puzzle. The page is just waiting to be filled up.

The more elements you give to the desktop designer to squeeze onto the page, the better. Of course there's a limit. You can only reduce the type size so far or it will become unreadable. You can use some tricks to maximize the allotted space. Condensed typefaces will get more words on the page.

Three columns versus two will accommodate more text on a page. If you didn't realize this, try it, you'll be surprised. There's a rule of thumb that says wider columns of type need more leading. This helps the eye stay on the right line.

Graphic Design

Graphic design is vastly different from desktop design. The designer looks at the blank page as a waiting canvas. A piece of art is the ultimate goal. Something readable, but something that starts the reader's juices flowing. The page is no longer a puzzle, because the designer is not puzzled.

There are two words that separate the graphic designer from the desktop designer: *white space!* The graphic designer loves it, but it bothers the desktop designer who loves to fill every corner of the page.

There are two words that separate the graphic designer from the desktop designer: white space!

As an example of this, I've prepared several layouts showing what happens when a desktop design meets a graphic designer. The copy is made up and is only meant to show volume. The object of this exercise is to show how less can be more. The initial layout is competent and gets the job done.

What happens when graphic designers have copy and illustrative elements taken away? They love it. This is a real-world problem and happens all the time. Any designer working with a publication may have to work with less if the editor cuts things.

A good designer could take one word or one sentence and fill an entire page. But don't forget, part of that filler is white space. If you are representing a design firm, you may wish to have your design staff produce a set of layouts similar to those shown on the following pages. I'm sure your company has had some publications where the page or pages were packed.

If your company is into desktop design, market what they do best and accumulate their best samples. Whether you're selling Cadillacs or Chevys, there's a customer for you.

The Real News

All the Real News Fit To Print   *May 2000*

Real News Debut

Consectetur adipscing elit, sed diam nonnumy eiusmod tempor incidunt ut labore et dolore magna aliquam eret volupat. Ut enim ad minimim veniami quis nostrud exercitation ullamcorpor suscipit ea commodo consequat. Duis autem vel emun irure dolor

Charts Are Art

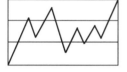

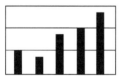

in reprehenderit in voluptate velit esse molestaie son consequat, vel illum dolore eu fugiat nulla pariatur.

At vero eos et accusam it iusto odio dignissim qui blandit praesent lupatum delenit aigue duos dolor et molestias exceptur sint occaecat cupidtat non provident, simil tempor sunt in culpa qui officia deserunt mollit anim id est laborum et dolor fugai Et harumd

dereud facilis est erexpedit distinct.

Nam liber a tempor cum soluta nobis eligend option comgue nihil quod a impedit anim id quod maxim placeat facer possim omnis et voluptas assumedna est, omnis dolor repellend. Tempo rem alutem quinusd et aur office debit aut tum rerum necessit in atib saepe eveniet ut er repudiand sint et molestia non este recusand. Itaque earud rerum hic tenetury sapiente delectus au aut prefer endis dolorib asperiore repellat.

Hanc ego cum tene sentntiam, quid est cur verear ne ad eam non possing accommodare nost ros quos tu paulo ante cum memorite it tum etia ergat. Nos amice et nebevol, olestias access potest fier ad augendas cum conscien to

factor tum poen ldgum odioque civiuda. Et tamen in busda taneque pecun modut est neque nonor imper ned libiding gen epular religuard on cupiditat quas nulla praid om umdant.

Improb pary minuiti potius inflammad ut coercent magist and et dodecendense videantur. Invitat igitur vera ration bene santos ad iustitiami aequitated fidem. Neque hominy infant aut inuiste fact est cond que neg facile efficerd possit duo conteud notiner si effecerit, et opes vel fortunag vel ingen liberalitat magis om conveniunt, da but tutung benefolent sib conciliant et, al aptissim est ad quiet.

Endium caritat praesert cum omning null sit caus peccand quaeret en imigent cupidat a natura proficis facile explent sine

Special News

Nam liber a tempor cum soluta nobis eligend option comgue nihil quod a impedit anim id quod maxim placeat facer possim omnis et voluptas assumedna est, omnis dolor repell end. Tem orem alutem quinusd et aur office debit aut tum rerum necessit in atib saepe eveniet ut er repudiand sint et molestia non este recusand.

The layout shown above, in greek type, is our starting point. The elements have been placed in a typical and competent desktop design. The editor asks that a photo be added with a two-line caption, and the editor says the amount of copy will stay the same.

The Real News

All the Real News Fit To Print   *May 2000*

Real News Debut

Consectetur adipscing elit, sed diam nonnumy eiusmod tempor incidunt ut labore et dolore magna aliquam eret volupat. Ut enim ad minimim veniami quis nostrud exercitation ullamcorpor suscipit ea commodo consequat. Duis autem vel emun irure dolor in reprehenderit in voluptate velit esse

Charts Are Art

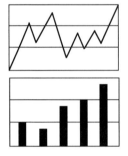

molestaie son consequat, vel illum dolore eu fugiat nulla pariatur.

At vero eos et accusam it iusto odio dignissim qui blandit praesent lupatum delenit aigue duos dolor et molestias exceptur sint occaecat cupidtat non provident, simil tempor sunt in culpa qui officia deserunt mollit anim id est laborum et dolor fugai Et harumd dereud facilis est erexpedit distinct.

Nam liber a tempor cum soluta nobis eligend option comgue nihil

quod a impedit anim id quod maxim placeat facer possim omnis et voluptas assumedna est, omnis dolor repellend. Tempo rem alutem quinusd et aur office debit aut tum rerum necessit in atib saepe eveniet ut er repudiand sint et molestia non este recusand. Itaque earud rerum hic tenetury sapiente delectus au aut prefer endis dolorib asperiore repellat.

Hanc ego cum tene sentntiam, quid est cur verear ne ad eam non possing accommodare nost ros quos tu paulo ante cum memorite it tum etia ergat. Nos amice et nebevol, olestias access potest fier ad augendas cum conscien to factor tum poen ldgum odioque civiuda. Et tamen in busda taneque pecun modut est neque nonor imper ned libiding gen epular religuard on cupiditat quas nulla praid om umdant.

Improb pary minuiti potius inflammad ut coercent magist and et dodecendense videantur. Invitat igitur vera ration bene santos ad iustiti-

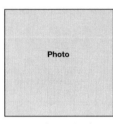

Tem orem alutem quinusd et aur office debit.

ami aequitated fidem. Neque hominy infant aut inuiste fact est cond que neg facile efficerd possit duo conteud notiner si effecerit, et opes vel fortunag vel ingen liberalitat magis om conveniunt, da but tutung benefolent sib conciliant et, al aptissim est ad quiet.

Endium caritat praesert cum omning null sit caus peccand quaeret en imigent cupidat a natura proficis facile explent sine

---

Special News

Nam liber a tempor cum soluta nobis eligend option comgue nihil quod a impedit anim id quod maxim placeat facer possim omnis et voluptas assumedna est, omnis dolor repell end. Tem orem alutem quinusd et aur office debit aut tum rerum necessit in atib saepe eveniet ut er repudiand sint et molestia non este recusand.

As I said, it's easy to add things. I've reduced the type from 12 pt. to 11 pt. The layout still doesn't look jammed. I've used up most of my white space, but the layout works. There are many other layout solutions available.

Real News

All the Real News Fit To Print   *May 2000*

Real News Debut

Consectetur adipscing elit, sed diam nonnumy eiusmod tempor incidunt ut labore et dolore magna aliquam eret volupat. Ut enim ad minimim veniami quis nostrud exercitation ullamcorpor suscipit ea commodo consequat. Duis autem vel emun irure dolor in reprehenderit in voluptate velit esse molestaie son consequat, vel illum dolore eu fugiat nulla pariatur.

At vero eos et accusam it iusto odio dignissim qui blandit praesent lupatum delenit aigue duos dolor et molestias excepteur sint occaecat cupidtat non provident, simil tempor sunt in culpa qui

officia deserunt mollit anim id est laborum et dolor fugai Et harumd dereud facilis est erexpedit distinct.

Nam liber a tempor cum soluta nobis eligend option comgue nihil quod a impedit anim id quod maxim placeat facer possim omnis et voluptas assumedna est, omnis dolor repellend. Tempo rem alutem quinusd et au aut tum rerum neco saepe eveniet ut er re et molestia non est Itaque earud rerum sapiente delectus au endis dolorib asperiore

Hanc ego cum ter quid est cur verear ne possing accommodare nost ros quos tu paulo ante cum memorite it tum etia ergat. Nos amice et nebevol, olestias access potest fier

Delete charts, picture, and copy as indicated.

—Editor

Special News

Nam liber a tempor cum soluta nobis eligend option comgue nihil quod a impedit anim id quod maxim placeat facer possim omnis et voluptas assumedna est, omnis dolor repell end. Tem orem alutem quinusd et aur office debit aut tum rerum necessit in atib saepe eveniet ut er repudiand sint et molestia non este recusand.

Now the challenge. The editor doesn't like the masthead design and wants to shorten the title to just Real News. *She has also cut the length of copy in both the text and boxed copy area.*

real **news**

*All the
Real News Fit
To Print.*

May 2000

Real News Debut

Consectetur adipscing elit, sed diam nonnumy eiusmod tempor incidunt ut labore et dolore magna aliquam eret volupat. Ut enim ad minimim veniami quis nostrud exercitation ullamcorpor suscipit ea commodo consequat. Duis autem vel emun irure dolor in reprehenderit in voluptate velit esse molestaie son consequat, vel illum dolore eu fugiat nulla pariatur.

At vero eos et accusam it iusto odio dignissim qui blandit praesent lupatum delenit aigue duos dolor et molestias exceptur sint occaecat cupidtat non provident, simil tempor sunt in culpa qui officia deserunt mollit anim id est laborum et dolor fugai Et harumd dereud facilis est erexpedit distinct.

Special News

Nam liber a tempor cum soluta nobis eligend option comgue nihil quod a impedit anim id quod maxim placeat facer possim omnis et voluptas assumedna est, omnis dolor repell end. Tem orem alutem quinusd et aur office debit aut tum rerum .

Nam liber a tempor cum soluta nobis eligend option comgue nihil quod a impedit anim id quod maxim placeat facer possim omnis et voluptas assumedna est, omnis dolor repellend. Tempo rem alutem quinusd et aur office debit aut tum rerum necessit in atib saepe eveniet ut er repudiand sint et molestia non este recusand. Itaque earud rerum hic tenetury

sapiente delectus au aut prefer endis dolorib asperiore repellat.

Hanc ego cum tene sentntiam, quid est cur verear ne ad eam non possing accommodare nost ros quos tu paulo ante cum memorite it tum etia ergat. Nos amice et nebevol, olestias access potest fier

Here is a new layout with less copy, no photo, and no charts. The use of white space is the only solution. Even the use of a box for the highlighted copy has been dropped. What will that editor do next?

74

news

*All the
Real News Fit
To Print.*

May 2000

Real News Debut

Consectetur adipscing elit, sed diam nonnumy eiusmod tempor incidunt ut labore et dolore magna aliquam eret volupat. Ut enim ad minimim veniami quis nostrud exercitation ullamcorpor suscipit ea commodo consequat. Duis autem vel emun irure dolor in reprehenderit in voluptate velit esse molestaie son consequat, vel illum dolore eu fugiat nulla pariatur.

At vero eos et accusam it iusto odio dignissim qui blandit praesent lupatum delenit aigue duos dolor et molestias exceptur sint occaecat cupidtat non provident, simil tempor sunt in culpa

qui officia deserunt mollit anim id est laborum et dolor fugai Et harumd dereud facili dit distinct.

Nam liber a tempor nobis eligend option nihil quod a impedit quod maxim placeat omnis et voluptas ass omnis dolor repellen rem alutem quinusd et aur office debit aut tum rerum necessit in atib saepe eveniet ut er repudiand sint et molestia non este recusand. Itaque earud rerum hic tenetury

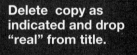

Delete copy as indicated and drop "real" from title.

—Editor

Now the final curveball is thrown. The editor is sadistic. She wants to drop the highlighted copy, a quarter of the text, and drop the word Real *from the title. Is this a test?*

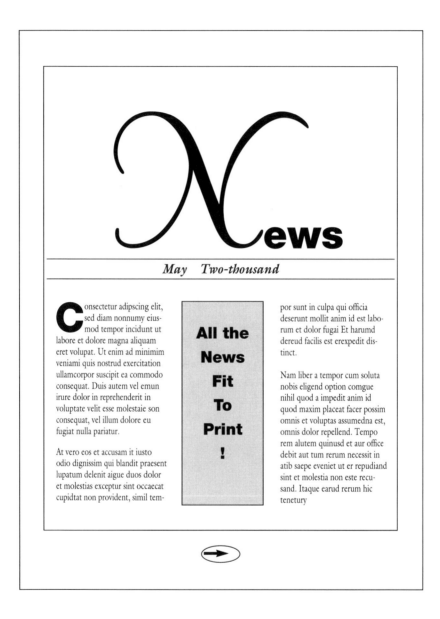

Designers love it. It's like Br'er Rabbit saying to Br'er Fox, "Please don't throw me in that briar patch." And when the fox throws him into it, he yells back, "I was born and raised in a briar patch." Try this with your Web page, too.

The Ultimate Challenge

The ultimate challenge comes from within. Clients and editors don't make changes to get us upset. It's generally poor planning or circumstances beyond their control that cause changes.

Desktop designers often say that they are problem-solvers. Graphic designers don't solve problems, but come up with solutions never imagined. There are many software packages for design, and they usually show a really great layout on the box. The manufacturer suggests that anyone can design a page like the one shown.

This is a little like showing a man next to a toolbox showing off a car he built. There's more to the product than just the tools. I've often said that there's a similarity between a graphic designer and an architect. There's also a similarity between a desktop designer and a draftsman.

The graphic designer is like an architect . . . the desktop designer is like a draftsman.

There is plenty of room for both types in the visual marketplace. The secret is to know what kind of clients you should be looking for and then to go after them. I also believe you should go after the best work in your company's area of expertise.

Here's one more example of the ultimate design challenge. What happens when suddenly you're left with only one line to fill an entire page. Sure, you could make the words big or just float them in the middle of the page, but would that compel the reader? I think not.

The line is: *design is a necessity, not a decoration*

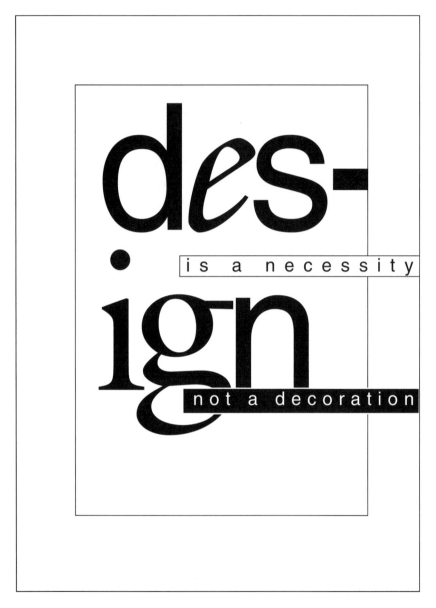

The solution is simple, yet planned. The design uses grids and various weights of black versus negative space to form a balance. It's not how much you say, it's how you say it.

CHAPTER 10

ELECTRONIC DESIGN
TECHNOLOGY CAN HELP YOU
CLOSE THE SALE

This chapter is not meant to intimidate you, so I'll stick to the basics. *The computer age is here and everyone is in it for good.* There's no turning back. At this writing, there are a few designers who refuse to use a computer. They believe the computer has killed good design. I beg to differ with them. Bad designers have hurt electronic design.

In many cases, the problems of the new technology are those of perception. I was interviewed by phone and was asked how the computer has affected my business. Most of the questions were leading and told me exactly what the interviewer thought. I was asked: "Were clients making more changes because the computer would allow them to? Was the capital investment in new equipment hurting my cash flow? Had the quality of design declined because of the electronics? Did I feel the printing industry was receiving inferior electronic files from designers?" I could only answer from my own perspective, and the answer was "no" on all counts. It seemed the interviewer had her mind made up.

It reminded me a bit of the story of the blind men and the elephant. Each of the blind men described his perception of the elephant by the part he was touching. One of the men touching the elephant's leg said, "The elephant is like a tree." Another man held the elephant's tail and exclaimed, "No, an elephant is like a snake." Each man was partially correct from his own vantage point, but his knowledge of the whole picture would be forever lacking. This is human nature. We only believe what we perceive.

Show Your Client How to Save Money

The major advantage of computer-aided design is the lack of the need for traditional typesetting. Re-keyboarding is no longer necessary so mistakes are fewer and labor is less intense. In the past, if the designer's specifications changed, the typesetter would have to retype all of the text. This was costly and could cause errors. Now, the designer imports the client's copy into a layout and there is no new keyboarding. This saves time and time is money.

Costly Mistakes Your Client Can Avoid

If you walk your clients through the stages of the design and production process, you can show them where they can save money. Start by reviewing the schedule with your client. The schedule should clearly spell out each phase of a project. In going over it together, you will see immediately what ground is unfamiliar to your client and will be able to offer guidance. The schedule is a friend of everyone involved in a project. It generates questions and keeps surprises to a minimum.

The schedule is a friend...
It generates questions and keeps surprises
to a minimum.

Proofreading is an art and proofreading marks need to be applied correctly. Copy marked with confusing directions will cause alteration charges. And, no client likes these. The most costly error, though, is when the client makes changes on his or her original disk and not on the hard copy. This means the designer will need to re-do the entire layout. To avoid this, explain the process to your client up front.

Once the client approves the page proofs, the designer's disk is given to the printer. The printer will generate film directly from the designer's disk. This bypasses the old step of having art boards photographed and negatives made. This saves time and there are less chances of foreign materials blemishing the negatives. There is one drawback for the client. The machine generated negatives are not easily spot corrected. If one small correction is marked, a complete new negative will have to be pulled. This means the client should take extra care in the earlier proofing stages.

Next, a blueline is pulled just like before. From here on, the printing process is similar to the way it always has been. Yes, there are waterless presses and computerized consoles on the printing presses. There are five-, six-, seven-, and eight-color presses, but it's still ink on paper.

CHAPTER 11

SELLING WEB SITE DESIGN

To sell Web page design, you must be selling design, not technology, not programming, and especially not pretty pictures. If you represent a company that specializes in design, this chapter will help you understand why "design" is the key word, not publication, annual report, corporate identity or advertising design.

The Internet is changing even as I write this chapter. This means you have to be aware of what is new, what works, what doesn't work, and what has been discarded. The Internet is a simple concept that appears to be a miracle cure for all communications. This couldn't be further from the truth. It is a jungle and it can be a bottomless money pit. Your success will come from guiding your client through this jungle.

The Internet Frontier

In 1995 the main "surfers" (those wandering around on the Worldwide Web) were for the most part eighteen- to twenty-five-year-old males. There were a handful of companies fighting to get you to subscribe to their service plans. These are called "service providers." Each offered a set number of hours of free time with additional hours at a special rate. Competition got fierce, and the amount of free time was constantly being increased to get you, a potential customer, online. Small service providers cropped up offering bare-bones plans. These would get you online, but after that you were on your own.

Business Finds the Internet

In the next several years businesses felt they had to have a presence on the Internet. No matter what the field, competitors would use their Web site as a talking point to show they were on the leading edge of technology. Many of the pages created by Web designers were nothing more than ads with a twist, and the twist was that you could see their ad on your computer.

As designers got more savvy, the ads got more sophisticated, but they still had one basic flaw. Even if someone visited the site once, why would they come back? And if the site did provide new information on a regular basis, who would update the information so it was timely?

A Web page can be a very expensive investment, and like any business investment, it can be a success or a bust. Doing homework applies to this investment as much as any other. The more you know about your clients' competition, their niche audience, and which products or services they offer are the most marketable, the more you will be able to make design suggestions that are relevant to their marketing budgets.

Electronic Mail

Probably the biggest reason business embraces the Internet is eletronic mail (e-mail). There are companies that are on the Internet only because of the necessity of being able to send and receive e-mail. This is true within the industry of printing. Small print shops have always kept one eye open to see what the big guys were up to.

Most of the independent quick print shops are owned by people who are not lovers of computers. The individuals running these shops watched computers wipe out typographers and later many service bureaus. The computer seemed to be the villain and they even felt it might someday threaten their own livelihood by somehow replacing the printed page. Now the Internet is another communication method that doesn't need paper.

Since designers were quick to see the potential of e-mail, they embraced the process as another way to communicate faster with clients, printers, and prepress houses. For printers, ignoring e-mail was a little like ignoring fax machines. And none of these communication tools seemed to go away. They got more important as well as more dependable. The market and the client were in the driver's seat.

Printers watched in horror as some other fundamental industries collapsed before their eyes. Looking back at the early computers setting type, the professional typographers were correct in their criticism of the typeset product generated by those early design computers. The type that was set was, in many cases, inferior in the proportions of the letters, and tracking defaults were often uneven.

For printers, ignoring e-mail was a little like ignoring fax machines.

Nowadays, however, we remember the first airplane and its short flight, compared with contemporary supersonic travel. It was obvious to everyone but the typesetter that the technology would not only catch up with but surpass traditional type. Today we, as designers, can set type in single point increments. With the fonts redesigned by new masters, the art of typography is as strong as one's imagination. Printers themselves concede that the Internet is indispensable for sending and receiving data files. And, as did the airplane, Web communication will continue to evolve.

Selling Web Pages

Before you can design Web pages for others, you must develop your own site. It needs to be your showpiece until you've added clients to your portfolio. You must understand basic marketing and this may take some night courses. We have already stressed that a Web page has to be more than pretty images advertising your client's wares. This alone could put you ahead of your competition.

Let's set our priorities as to what a Web page needs to achieve. The goals are pretty simple. If one is to spend money on marketing, one wants to know what return to expect. However, it is going to be tough to be precise because the Internet is still in its infancy. Your client may have knowledge that would be of public interest, in which case a page that functioned as a civic information service might be in order. The company that has this page is a sponsor of good news and always a winner in good taste.

What if there is nothing tangible to sell? If your client has no product except a service such as law, accounting, or even plumbing, you might design the home page as a historical perspective on the profession. This can prove educational; give the client the image of a champion of his field.

What if there is a product line but budget won't allow for all of the products to be shown or listed? You can design an elaborate opening page with teasers. Display the hottest items or the best values, and make the page revolve around these items.

What can be done on a bare-bones budget? Something very creative and well-designed doesn't have to come with a big price tag. Establish links to and from sites in complementary trades that will send customers to your client's page.

What turns off pro surfers (those surfing for commerce, not fun)? There are some taboos that will never go away. Follow these don'ts.

1. Don't create a slow-to-load, but beautiful page. As with a print ad, people don't want to spend too much time reading—or waiting to read.

2. Don't talk down to your reader. Each page should reflect the level of your client's sophistication.

3. Don't overuse animation. It may look like a neat gimmick, but in many cases that's all it is.

4. Don't just create a colorful Yellow Pages ad. At the present time, the Web is not a big phone book. There already is a phone book and its easier to use. This does not apply to including your client on a Web Yellow Page site provided by the phone company.

5. Don't shotgun. If your clients have only one location in a rural area, there is no reason for them to have an expensive global presence.

6. Don't serve up a vanity page. Just because your client wants one doesn't mean it is the best exposure for the money. Some other designer will come up with a way to send out an effective message, and your client will be theirs. And don't forget, you probably are doing other graphics for this account, which you could lose as well.

7. Don't offer a proposal to design a page if you are not sure of all of the technical support you will need. Shooting from the hip can be very dangerous to all involved.

There are many more don'ts and I know they will multiply as this industry grows. One important thing to remember is: your client's Web page will be easier for your competition to access than, say, a corporate brochure. Don't be surprised when some competitor redesigns part of your client's page (with just enough style to titillate) and you have to respond.

An Interview with a Leader on the Leading Edge

The following is an interview with John Waters, president of Waters Design Associates in New York. John is an award-winning designer on the cutting edge of computer-generated design. He started with a Lightspeed design system in the early eighties, and he has made his mark in producing award-winning annual reports and corporate graphics for Fortune 500 companies.

Several years ago, John entered the infant design field of the Worldwide Web. His firm has since quadrupled in size, he has moved to new and larger office space, and he has become a leading force in Web site design. The following interview was conducted by phone and gives us some insight into John's perceptions of where all this is going.

Sparkman: What is different between selling Web site design and graphic design?

Waters: The big difference is technology. As a graphic designer, you need to know how to produce what you design. The more you know, the more valuable you are to your client and the more money you make. This holds true whether you are working in print or on the Internet.

Sparkman: In general, describe the Internet marketplace for designers.

Waters: There are two basic levels. First, there is the small stand-alone site, which may be no more than twenty to forty pages. This is basically an information site. This type of low-level site can be designed with some off-the-shelf tools. Popular software like PageMill, NetObjectsFusion, or FrontPage are available for this level of site design. This might be compared to doing some small print projects like newsletters.

The other level is the large Web site that may have hundreds and hundreds of pages. It may have its own search engine, connect to a database, or connect to other corporate sites. It may connect by intranets or Legacy Systems. It may have templates or dynamically generated pages. For that you need a different set of tools and a lot more knowledge about the Web. Our basic programming tool is BB Edit.

With the larger sites, you need to use a mix of different languages. CGI, Java, JavaScript, PearlScript, and C++ are just a few.

Sparkman: What kind of capital investment is needed for gearing up for Web site design?

Waters: Here again there are two ways to look at this. On the low end, the cost to access the Web is minimal. The basic software programs are in the $500 range so you could be up and running for less than $5,000. On the other hand, if you are going to design large sites, you can spend a lot of money. The biggest cost is programming talent. You need people who can do things in HTML. This type of person in New York charges around $50 per hour. With advanced languages like CGI, PearlScript, and Java, you may pay $100–150 per hour. For software development you can pay $200–300 per hour.

We work with other groups as alliances so we can offer complete packages of services, but we must know enough to communicate with these partners. This is much like a traditional design firm's production manager who coordinates the complete production of a project.

Another investment is the cost of additional equipment. You have to beta test on different platforms with different browsers. You need to see your work on a PC, or a UNIX with Internet Explorer 3 and 4, or Netscape 3.4 and 4.0. Beta testing is time-consuming and expensive, but you need to thoroughly test a site before it goes public.

We set up what we call a "sandbox," which is a site that people can access with a password but is not open to the public. We test it here and we have other people test it outside. The site will be accessed on other platforms to see how it holds up. We may have to develop different files to be read off of a Mac or PC.

Sparkman: What do you handle within your studio and what do you send out?

Waters: We have designers, producers, programmers, and technicians working in the studio. Beta site testing is often an outside function. But with the exception of heavy engineering requirements, most of our work is performed in the studio.

Sparkman: Can a design studio handle both print and Web design effectively under the same roof?

Waters: Yes. But it does, for the most part, take different people for each. I do have some print designers who can also design Web sites. For the most part, they tend to be stronger in one or the other.

Last year we were 65 percent new media. Some was CD but the majority was Web work. We're trying to keep a balance—I don't want to lose print. And we are finding that with the development of Web sites, there is often a need for printed materials. Direct mail is used to drive the public to a site.

Sparkman: Have you found that your print clients were ready for you to take them onto the Web as a natural evolution?

Waters: Actually, no. Some clients have said, "We know you do Web work, but that's not the same as someone who does Web work exclusively." They want to know they are talking to an engineer who can talk technically. For the most part we've done quite well, but every so often there will be a client who wants a pure technology firm.

Sparkman: Can't you use your strength in design and marketing communications as a major plus over technology companies?

Waters: Yes, we do and that has been a successful route to take. And it's the truth. We like to say we use all media to communicate for our clients. We bring strategic communications thinking to the table, not just technology.

We are also using the Internet to show both Web site development and print layouts. We set up a "workroom" where clients can come and see the layouts. With a conference call we can talk and respond interactively as if we were in the same conference room in the same office. We can make changes or revisions on the fly.

Last year we developed a monthly newsletter for a major telecommunications company. After the initial concept layouts were approved, we went on line and showed finished pages in a workroom, and then sent the okayed files to the printer, electronically.

Sparkman: Are there any pricing guidelines for Web site design?

Waters: It's all over the place. Several years ago we looked at a site of forty to fifty pages with the same pricing formula as an annual report. At the time, an annual report was $1,000 a page. But there are sites that are five hundred to a thousand pages and we can't charge by that page rate.

The way we estimate is like we always have—by the hour. We have established rates for different functions, i.e., designers, producers, programmers, etc. Each rate is based on salary cost times a multiple which includes overhead and profit.

Sparkman: Do you see the Internet replacing print?

Waters: No, not entirely. There will be catalogs that may go on line without a printed companion piece. With the expense of printing a catalog, it makes economical sense to put it on a Web site and update it as necessary. Portability will be the key to how far the Internet will go in replacing other media. If someone can access the Web from a remote site, with a portable hand-held independent unit, you may see a lot of print disappear. It is hard to predict what technology will bring us tomorrow.

This concluded our interview. It is obvious that design is here to stay, whether it be print or Web site development. Selling design will remain a multifaceted job requiring skills from various disciplines.

This book remains print-oriented, for the most part, because, at this time, print remains the dominant medium. And, even though Web display is developing in ways that are different from design for the printed page, parallels between these two areas exist. The process of buying illustration for Web sites is much the same as purchasing it for graphic designs. A Web site may require that you proofread a client's script, just as page layout requires you to proof the copy. The basic terminology of the business has not changed; it is the communication tool used every day.

CHAPTER 12

PROOFREADING
YOUR CLIENT'S WORK LIKE
A PRO

Proofreading is a necessity in working with clients. If you have to review anything written, you need to know how to mark up a proof. You may be the president of your design company, but you still have to communicate. Use of the correct proofreading marks communicates in a universal language, leaving nothing to chance.

To understand proofreading, you must know the fundamentals of type. Type is set in point sizes. Each typeface has special characters, enabling it to handle most any situation. Any one size and style of type is considered a "font." Lowercase letters are the small characters, and uppercase are the capital letters. The typographers of old used to keep the letters in two cases. The top one held the capital letters, thus called uppercase, and the bottom held what we call the lowercase.

ABC is a serif type style.

ABC is a sans-serif type style.

There are two basic type styles. They are serif and sans serif. Sans serif means without serifs, which are little "feet" at the tops and bottoms of letters. This book is set in serif type.

There is an ongoing battle over the readability of sans-serif versus serif type. I was told once by a righteous editor that I should not use sans-serif type because it was not readable, and that I should never reverse type out of a color (reverse is the use of white type on a black or color background). I asked this editor if the U.S. Department of Transportation had a death wish for the American public because most of our signs on the nation's interstates have reversed sans-serif letters.

Photocopy the page
with the proofreading marks and
keep it where your proofing is
generally done.

On the following pages we will look at the basics of proofreading copy and effectively marking the corrections. To avoid changes being overlooked, use a contrasting ink color and mark changes in the margin. Don't be afraid of writing a note if you feel the proofreading marks are too cryptic. After all, you are not trying to show off your new skills, you're trying to communicate. This same rule holds true in marking up a printer's proof. You should be as straightforward as possible. If you don't know certain printing terms, don't try to fake it. Use everyday English to explain what you want to see. Also, don't be afraid to draw a sketch or diagram of what you want. Printers don't want to guess any more than you want them to.

Photocopy the page with the proofreading marks. Keep it where your proofing is generally done. Remember, proofreading is an art. People are paid to proofread. These people are professional editors. Like them, you must know how to communicate your thoughts.

Your client may be a professional editor or writer, but there will come a time when you'll be working with a novice. You can be a great aid if you can help by using the correct proofreading marks.

Proofreading Symbols

caps	All caps	*lc*	Lower CASE
	Apostrophe/single quote	⊔	Lower words or letters
bf	Boldface	flush ¶	No indent
✗	Broken type	ok w/c	Okay with corrections
	Close quotes		Open quotes
	Close up space	¶	Paragraph
∴ or :⎮	Colon	(|)	Parenthesis
	Comma	⊙	Period
/–/	Dash	?/	Question mark
	Delete/close up	⊓	Raise words or letters
	Delete/remove	rom	*Roman* type
▢	Em space/indent	no ¶	Run in
⟨…⟩	Ellipsis	;⎮	Semicolon
!/	Exclamation point	sc	Small caps
⌐	Flush left	(sp)	Spell out
⌐	Flush right	tr	Transpose letters
═	Horizontally align	‖	Vertically align
=	Hyphen	wf	Wrong font
stet	Ignore marks		
cap	Initial caps		
#	Insert space		
ital	Italicize		
ls	Letter space		
lf	Lightface		

Proofing Copy

Example:

cap
⊂

these paragraphs have bene set to give you an
example of how proof reading marks work. Note
that both sides of the copy block are used for the
marks.

no¶
˅

It is important to know ho to use *these* marks
correctly, because they're universal in communicating instructions.

wf

Now that everyone can typeset on a computer, it
is more important than ever to the use correct
proofredding symbols. Practice corecting copy you

9/a
lc
⊔

RECEIVE without looking at the examples to see
how much you've retained.

cap

This copy does not contain all of the marks we
have covered. i have used the ones most common

⊙

to give you a feel for what a "marked-up" page
would look like. The methods for using the rest of
the marks should be apparent from what has been
marked here.

tr

lf

w/ rom
∧

#
tr
r
∧

⊓

=
∧

𝒴

Proofed Copy

Example:

These paragraphs have been set to give you an example of how proofreading marks work. Note that both sides of the copy block are used for the marks. It is important to know how to use these marks correctly because they're universal in communicating instructions.

Now that everyone can typeset on a computer, it is more important than ever to use the correct proofreading symbols. Practice correcting copy you receive without looking at the examples to see how much you've retained.

This copy does not contain all of the marks we have covered. I have used the ones most common to give you a feel for what a "marked-up" page would look like. The methods for using the rest of the marks should be apparent from what has been marked here.

A minimum of two people should proof the blueline: one from your company and one from the client's company. Beyond that, try to have as few people as possible review it. The more important the project is, the more true this becomes.

There is an exception to every rule. I designed an annual report for a major corporation. When the blueline was presented to the president, he was on his way to Europe for an emergency meeting. He took the blueline on the airplane with him, and for seven hours he scrutinized every word in it. When I got it back, the entire annual report required a new layout and had to be reset.

This was not only time consuming, but very expensive. If you are ever working on an annual report for a company, remember that it is the president's message to the stockholders. All of the corporate palace guards' opinions mean nothing if the president doesn't agree. Be sure the right people see and sign off on the copy before it goes to the printer.

CHAPTER 13

BUYING ILLUSTRATION AND PHOTOGRAPHY FOR YOUR CLIENT

There are common-sense rules that apply to the art of buying illustration and photography. Whether it is to be used in print or on the Internet, the rules are pretty much the same. Budget is probably the biggest constraint. After all, if you had unlimited funds you could hire LeRoy Neiman or Annie Leibovitz and win all kinds of awards. Unfortunately, it's the real world. Most of us have to beg, borrow, or steal to get funds for illustration or photography. Somehow, these elements appear to most clients to be the icing on the proverbial cake.

Start a Morgue

Start a morgue, not the kind that holds dead bodies. A morgue is a file or files containing reference materials. In this case, your morgue will contain books on current stock photography, illustrators and reps, special effects, retouchers, and old engravings.

Let's start with illustration. You will probably receive mailings from illustrators or their representatives. If you are new to the field or your company has just created your position for selling design, you may need some help in getting started. Join the local Art Directors Club. Usually those clubs are run by volunteers who are designers. There may be an Illustrators Club in your area and this is an even better way to get sources. Also, a local chapter of the American Institute of Graphic Arts (AIGA) can be of assistance. If you're in a remote area, you can contact the national headquarters of the AIGA. Their address is listed in appendix 2, "Professional Organizations and Publications That Can Help You."

One of the best ways to work with illustrators is through companies that represent several different artists with different styles. You can discuss budget, concept, and schedule with a representative, who can recommend the best illustrator for your project. Sometimes this can be a big plus because you don't have to bring these delicate topics into your conversation with the artist you have chosen to work with.

Don't be afraid of logistics. I've worked with illustrators on the other side of the country. With fax machines, you can receive rough layouts as quickly as if the illustrator were in the same city. In fact, often quicker than I used to receive them before fax machines. Once your client approves the sketch, the final illustration can be sent to you overnight.

Finding Photographers and Illustrators

Photography is an art. It's best to have reviewed the portfolios of as many photographers as possible. They'll beat down your door once they know your company is a buyer. But, if you're in a remote area, get a copy of *Corporate Showcase* (also in appendix 2). This publication, and the others listed in this book, will give you miniportfolios of photographers, as well as of illustrators and designers all over the country. If you're in a large metropolitan area, there may be local sourcebooks available.

For a listing of professional photographers, contact the American Society of Media Photographers (ASMP) in your area. If there is no local ASMP, the national headquarters address is also listed in appendix 2. Once the word is out that you're a buyer, you'll be on mailing lists and get tons of photographer's promos. These are excellent to carry around so you can show your client who's best at what. But do your homework. Find out what each photographer's day rate is. This way you can work with your client's budget.

How is Location Photography Bought?

The majority of location photographers charge by the day. This is called their "day rate," and usually doesn't include any expenses. All you get is the person behind the camera. Their assistant, travel, food, lodging, film, and processing are all extra. It's best to get an estimate of what the photographer feels will be incurred. Also, photographers limit the usage of their photos. You must negotiate if you want unlimited usage. Your client's photos may also be sold as stock by the photographer after they use them unless you have made an agreement to the contrary. The photographer's estimate should spell out these conditions, but again, your purchase order can contradict them. If the photo subjects include people, make sure the photographer gets signed releases from everyone.

Location photographers can also charge by the photograph. If this is the case, there are probably still expenses not included in the fee. Here again, get an estimate of the expenses and a usage agreement. Remember, everything is negotiable. Don't let anyone dictate terms you feel are unfair. But remember, everything must be agreed upon, in writing, before the assignment starts, not after.

If the location photography is part of a graphic design project and a layout has been produced, the designer should, if at all possible, art direct the photography on location. This will ensure that the graphic feeling within the layout is maintained.

Is Studio Photography Different from Location?

Studio photography is similar to location. The same principles apply to estimates. Studio photography is usually billed by the image. With assignments such as catalogs, either a day rate or a cost per picture can be used. You must again discuss your client's use of the photos with the photographer.

Stock Photography: The Good and the Bad

The good part of using stock photography is that there are no hidden expenses from a photographer. The fee charged for the stock photos is usually negotiable, and will vary according to the type of publication, number of copies printed, whether the photo is on the cover, the size at which the photo will be used, and a number of other variables.

The downside to stock is that the photo may have been used before by someone else. Also, it may be difficult to find the exact photo of what your client wants. Stock photos can cost anywhere from a couple hundred dollars to a thousand or more. Most stock photo companies charge a minimum of fifteen hundred dollars if a photo is lost. This is because the photo they send to you is the original, not a duplicate. If a stock house sends you thirty slides to review and something happens to them, you're out forty-five thousand dollars. Make sure your insurance covers your exposure.

The Bettmann Archive offers a sourcebook of old photographs, engravings, and reproductions of paintings. These images are sold in the same way as other stock photographs. There are other sources for older photographs, but Bettman has made themselves the major source for the design industry.

CHAPTER 14

SELECTING A PRINTER FOR YOUR CLIENT

If you are involved in the management of your client's account, you may have to provide some print management, or buy their printing direct. As I mentioned earlier, I prefer to manage for an hourly fee instead of brokering these services.

No matter what you do, you must know about printing. After all, the final phase of graphic design is printing. (Unless your company is strictly into multimedia.) Even if you have a print buyer within your company, you will have to discuss printing with your client.

Selecting a printer sounds simple. So why devote a chapter to it? All you do is get out the phone book and look up a printer. There are probably plenty of them if you are in a metropolitan area. In a small town you have fewer to choose from locally, but in the age of the fax machine, computer modems, and overnight delivery services, out-of-town printers are easily accessible.

Printers are as different as people, because they are people. But printing plants usually operate in similar ways, because their managers have come from other printing plants, bringing with them some bad habits as well as some valuable improvements. You need to get to know the strong suits of the various printers in your area or the ones your client's company uses. Just like restaurants, some offer a great product while others offer good service. Look for the ones that offer both.

The Types of Printers Your Client Will Need

There are three or four types of printers that can serve your client's basic needs. You'll need a small quick-print shop for simple one-color jobs. Look for a commercial printer who recognizes that business printing is always time-driven, instead of a large chain, which usually caters to casual, walk-in customers. Word-of-mouth referrals are the best. If you can find another company similar to yours in size and in your general area, their production manager has probably found a good source and will be happy to share it with you. (That is, unless you're in direct competition.)

You should not only interview printing salespeople, you should also meet their customer service representative (CSR).

One- and Two-Color Sheetfed

Once you have a quick-print source, your client will probably need printers who specialize in two-color work. In this age of tight budgets, most corporate and association printing is one or two colors. These same printers may be able to handle some four-color needs as well, if they have a mix of two- and four-color presses. Finding these printers to bid on projects is best done through the referral process.

You should not only interview the printing salespeople, but also meet their customer service representative (CSR). This is the person with whom you're going to spend the most time. The printing salespeople are constantly out making calls, so you need access to their in-house personal assistant.

The most frustrating thing a printing company can put in, in my opinion, is voice mail. Service organizations that have voice mail have abusers. When your client's project is on a tight deadline, you call the CSR because you urgently need an answer to a critical question. If they have voice mail, they will call you back, but by then you may be in a meeting with your client, and you can't take the call. This has gotten so bad that after the CSR's voice mail message, I have dialed zero for the operator to page the CSR and have gotten her voice mail. There is no substitute for human contact.

Four-Color Sheetfed

If your clientele produces high-end publications in four or more colors, you will need printers who specialize in this kind of work. Here again, the referral method is best. These printers may be able to handle your two-color needs as well. But be careful because the reverse is not always true. Some two-color printers will say they can handle four-color projects on a two-color press, but this is neither cost effective nor smart. If you manage printing, you may be required to press inspect jobs. It's impossible to effectively press inspect a four-color job when two colors are printed at two different times. If the first pass is dry, the second pass is the only one that can be controlled by the pressman. If there's a problem with the ink densities of the first pass, it's too late for a correction. With a four-color press, however, the pressman can adjust any of the colors at any time, which is especially crucial when flesh tones are involved.

Web Printers

With a publication, catalog, or annual report that is printed in large quantities, you will probably need printers who have web presses. These presses print on rolls of paper versus sheets, and they're very fast. Web papers are less expensive and make sense for long runs. Web presses print on both sides of the sheet at the same time. A word of warning though. It's best if the printers you choose have backup presses. Web presses are complicated machines and can break down. If this happens and your client's job is on a tight deadline, you need to make sure the printer can run the job on another press. There are large and small web presses. Find out which size web press is best suited for your client's publication.

In interviewing printers, I suggest you take a tour of the plant. This is not just for P.R., but to let you note several important things, such as: How busy are they? Who are their customers? How advanced is their prepress area? Do they have proper facilities for press checks (meaning an area other than the press room with a light box for viewing proofs)? A printing plant's personality will show when you see it in action.

Press Inspections

Important projects often demand press inspections. Get yourself a printer's loupe, which is a magnifying glass that printers use to check registration and screen densities. You should also bring any previous proofs with you if the printer doesn't already have them there.

Press inspections are very important. They are sometimes referred to as "on-sites," or "press-checks." There is a psychological factor at work when a printer knows you are coming to check your job, and printers may even boast about catching problems before you arrive. When a job includes a press inspection, it automatically gains an added sense of importance.

There are some important rules to follow when you perform a press inspection. First, make sure all blueline corrections were made; it can be disastrous if you just assume that they were. Second, make sure you have all original color transparencies, artwork, and layouts with you where you are checking the press sheets. Third, look at color subjects upside down as well as right side up, so that the picture itself will not distract your eye from being objective. Check the registration. If there is a fifth or sixth PMS ink (color), make sure you have your own swatch and check the match on the sheet. The printer may have a PMS book that is old and the colors may not be as true as your own book. Fourth, if there are solid areas of color, ask the printer for a densitometer reading. This instrument, which looks like a big desk stapler, allows the pressman to check the amount of ink on the sheet. Last but not least, okay a sheet for the pressman, date it and sign it. Do the same thing for yourself because your copy can be crucial. I once had a designer come back from a press inspection *without* a duplicate of the okayed press sheet. Sure enough, the job was bad. We asked the printer if we could see the okayed press sheet. We were told it was lost, but it had been the same as the unacceptable final piece. We didn't have a leg to stand on. Don't let this happen to you!

CHAPTER 15

SELECTING PRINTING PAPERS FOR YOUR CLIENT

Appropriate choice of paper is the second most important part of a printed piece. Design is probably first, because a good design on the cheapest paper can still be effective. Knowing what papers are best suited for what types of printing projects is the only way to specify the best sheet for the job. There are many choices, but a knowledge of paper will narrow those choices down. For example, if a particular paper is very expensive but your print run is small (less than five thousand copies), the price of paper is not much of an overall cost factor in the printing price. On the other hand, if you're printing a large quantity (anything over five thousand copies) paper can be a significant cost factor. Paper's part of the total printing budget is a sliding one.

The "No-Brainer"

Selecting the right paper is an art form. You can limp along using the same papers over and over. No one will question you if your standby sheet is a good sheet. But many people, including award winning designers, use the same papers over and over again from laziness or lack of knowledge.

The computer has also been a perpetuator of designers using white coated papers, as these simulate the look of the papers used in the color printers generating full-color layouts.

The Paper Merchant

Paper merchants are wholesalers, and they can help you learn more about paper if you know how to use them. They stock a certain number of the popular papers. If a particular type of paper is not on their floor, they can usually get it overnight from the paper mill.

The relationship between the merchant and the mill has undergone some interesting changes over the years. Each merchant used to have exclusive rights to sell a certain mill's papers so that the competition was more between mills than merchants. The mills promoted their own papers through advertising and through mill trips, which enabled them to wine and dine printers and designers. In the seventies, however, the mills got smart and decided to make the merchants scramble. They gave more than one merchant in an area the right to sell their papers. Now each merchant usually represents several different mills.

To show you their stock, merchants make up boxes containing all of their samples, and you can get one from your local paper merchant's sales-promotion person. They will call on you and bring a fresh box, which is important because certain papers are discontinued, while others add new grades or change colors. This same representative will come in from time to time and upgrade the box. But remember, out of sight, out of mind. If you don't call every six months or so, he or she may forget to perform this service.

Paper Production—What You Need to Know

Paper is manufactured primarily from wood pulp. The wood is stripped of bark, ground up, and turned into usable pulp by means of heat, chemicals, or mechanical grinding. Once the pulp is in a semiliquid form, it is bleached. This gives the finished papers their brightness. Less bleaching leaves the paper browner, as in grocery bags. After bleaching, dyes and fillers are added to give the sheet a specific color and various properties such as rag content from cotton fibers or titanium oxide for opacity and brightness.

The modern papermaking machines are very complex, usually made up of three sections. First, the pulp is fed into the wet end. Then, it is forced into the second area, called the press section. Here the water is pressed out between rolls and felts. A dandy roll is used to compress the sheet and distribute the fibers. The dandy roll may carry a design on it to give the paper a watermark. In the third section, the product is dried to the desired level in a machine composed of steam-heated cast-iron drums. Now it has changed from a watery mush to paper that is recognizable as such. After this process, the paper is calendered, or finished. Coatings are added if the paper is to be a coated sheet.

Paper Characteristics

The Sheet: Paper has two sides. There is a wire side, which is the side of the sheet exposed to the wire in the press section. The other side is the felt side or top side, which was exposed to the dandy roll.

Paper Finish: This is the texture or smoothness of a sheet of paper. The usual finishes (from rough to smooth) are antique, eggshell, vellum, machine finished, and coated. Finishes can also be embossed onto the paper through the use of rotary embossing machines. Tweed, linen, and ribbed textures are just some of the patterns used.

I recently used a sheet named Champion Benefit Vertical Cover. The swatch book showed the sheet with grooves running up and down, so I assumed the the paper came that way. Most grooved or ribbed sheets are made with the the lines running horizontally. Since the name of the sheet was Vertical, I gave it no further thought.

I asked three printers for quotes on my printing specs. I received the prices and released the artwork (disk) to the low bidder. When the printer realized that, according to the layout specs, the grooves were supposed to run vertically, I was notified that there would be an extra cost of $225 because the grooves in the paper were actually horizontal. I was having the printing billed directly to my client, but I was charging for print management.

The printer said that he could not get as many covers out of a press sheet and more paper would be needed.

I was not happy. It had been my responsibility to get the quotes and I didn't feel I could call my client and ask for more money. I contacted the merchant and lodged a complaint. If the sheet had not been named Vertical Cover, I would've checked on the direction of the grooves. I am still waiting to hear if the mill is going to charge me for the difference.

Paper Coatings: A coating is a chemical applied to a sheet of paper to make it glossy. The coating can be on one or both sides of the sheet. If it's on one side only, it is called C1S ("C one S"). A sheet that is coated on two sides is C2S ("C two S").

Paper Grain: The grain is the direction of the fibers within a sheet. Folding against the grain often causes cracking. It is important to know how the grain runs in a sheet you're planning to print on and then fold. Your best source for this information is your paper merchant or your printer.

Paper Weights: The basis weight or paper weight, such as 80 pound text, is determined by the weight of five hundred sheets (a "ream") of the standard sheet size of 25×38 inches. Bond paper is based on a standard sheet size of 17×22 inches and a ream of 24 pound bond is roughly equivalent to 70 pound text. There are papers manufactured in Europe that are not standard American weights, but they offer variety and quality, and you can profit by knowing about them and their advantages.

Types of Papers

There are different types/grades of papers for different uses, which are often reflected in their names. Coated text and cover are used for the lion's share of four-color printing. Uncoated text and cover are the next up. Bond, book, offset, label, index, and newsprint are other grades used commercially. Designers can often add flair to a four-color piece by using an uncoated sheet of paper. Even metallics can be printed on uncoated papers.

Coated papers are best suited for higher quality jobs and may be gloss coated, dull coated, machine coated, and cast coated on one or two sides. Printing ink does not soak into a coated sheet as much as it does with an uncoated paper, so coated papers make halftones and color images look richer. Coated papers are associated with corporate capability brochures and annual reports. Since coated papers come in several grades and prices, you should not have to shy away from using them. Today, more and more coated papers are recycled, which also lowers their costs. The normal size of the sheet is 25 × 38 inches.

Uncoated papers (or text papers) can be excellent sheets for printing, and some are so smooth that it's hard to tell that they're not coated. (I don't like to refer to these sheets as text, because both coated and uncoated papers come in text and cover weights.) Uncoated papers are manufactured in many textures and colors. They can simulate flannel, linen, corduroy, or other textures. The normal sheet size for these papers is 25 × 38 inches as well.

Bond papers are used for stationery or forms; they take ink well from a typewriter or a pen. Part of this absorbency comes from the paper's rag content, which is the percentage of cotton fiber in a sheet of bond. Usually, 25 or 50 percent is the amount added. With the new laser printers, the fine letterhead papers are not as readily used because they jam up in the printers or soak up the ink. The sheet size is 17 × 22 inches, and trimmed to 8.5 × 11 inches.

Book papers are used, just as the name implies, for books and textbooks. These papers come in antique (rough) or smooth finishes. They also come in many weights, so that a book can be bulked up or down if need be. The sheet size is 25 × 38 inches.

Offset papers are similar to the coated and uncoated sheets used in letterpress printing, except that they have sizing added to resist the moisture that occurs in offset printing. The standard sheet size is 25 × 38 inches.

Index papers are stiff and take writing ink well, but are less expensive than cover grades. Index papers are used for cards or tabs and are used in place of the more expensive cover stocks. They come in a smooth or vellum (a little rougher) finish. The sheet sizes are 22.5 × 35 inches or 25.5 × 30 inches.

Newsprint papers, as their name suggests, are used for newspapers. The sheets are not as white as other papers, and ink tends to soak into them. Being relatively inexpensive, newsprint is ideal for large volumes of paper that modern newspapers need.

There are many great sheets of paper out there. Don't fall into a rut; try them. Your printer is your best consultant on the printability and economics of different papers.

Paper choice can make a major difference in the appearance of your finished job. A dull or plain design can be perked up with an exciting color or texture. But remember one thing: coated and smooth papers make pictures, whether color or black and white, look richer because the printing ink stands up on the sheet.

I once had a job on press that included a full-color image of an eagle that had originally been an engraving filled with delicate lines. I had chosen an uncoated white stock. While the printer was in make-ready, he used some coated sheets as waste. To my dismay, the eagle looked much brighter and more vibrant on the coated sheet than it did on the one I had chosen. I've never forgotten this lesson.

As I mentioned, this is not to say that halftones and color images can't look good on an uncoated sheet. It only means that you should be aware of the likely effect. When in doubt, call your local paper merchant and ask for the sample room. They can often find an example of the kind of printing you are contemplating on the sheet you want to use. If they can't, there may be a good reason why. Once again, as in printing, no one wants to be surprised by how a sheet will react to ink.

There are electronic and conventional methods of proofing on the stock in question. Check with a service bureau on what's available to you and your client. Some projects may be so high-profile that they justify a press proof.

Choosing Envelopes

When used, the envelope is an important complement to the printed piece. I've heard it said that most business people never see the envelope, because a secretary opens it and then throws it into the trash before the recipient gets to see it. But this is actually more the exception than the rule. Let's face it, most people in middle management don't have secretaries.

My theory is that a good envelope will often save the entire piece from the trash can. How many times has an envelope compelled you to open it? Publisher's Clearing House has certainly learned this secret.

Envelopes come in many standard sizes, mostly in white wove or kraft stocks. There are also envelopes in different colors and textures that are stocked by the paper merchants. If you have a project requiring a special envelope, or if you wish the printing to run across the folds, you can have the envelope converted or manufactured. You should allow more time for this process and budget a little more money. Here again, let the printer be your consultant.

There are wall charts available from envelope companies showing the different styles and sizes of their envelopes. I suggest getting one of these and taping it on the back of a door that's usually open. A merchant who stocks Strathmore papers should be able to get you an Old Colony envelope wall chart. Old Colony specializes in nothing but envelopes and is the leader in the industry.

If you're in an area without a local merchant, you can contact Old Colony directly at *Old Colony Envelopes, 94 N. Elm Street, Westfield, MA 01086. Phone: 1-800-343-1273.*

Styles of Envelopes

Envelopes are used for everyday correspondence or for very important direct mail campaigns. The importance of the envelope is naturally governed by its contents. I have seen envelopes made out of coated papers as well as fine linen. A word of caution: some papers do not take glue well. Check with your local paper merchant on a specific sheet's ability to be converted into an envelope.

Baronial Envelopes are used for formal invitations and announcements. They are usually white, and they are identified by their different sizes with an *A* prefix, such as A7 or A8.

Wallet Flap/Bankers Flap Envelopes are used for heavy-duty purposes because they will hold materials too bulky for regular envelopes.

Commercial Envelopes are made in bond or kraft papers. They are used for everyday business correspondence. The standard business envelope is the #10, which holds an 8.5 × 11–inch sheet of paper or standard company stationery. This size is also used for 4 × 9–inch direct mail brochures that are folded from a sheet of paper that is 9 × 12 inches into six panels.

Gusseted/Expansion Envelopes are used for bulky items. This type of envelope has a gusset, which is extra paper that folds out to accommodate the contents.

Open-Side/Booklet Envelopes have flaps on the long side. For instance, if an open-side envelope is 9 × 12 inches, it will open on the 12-inch side.

Open-End/Catalog Envelopes are just the opposite of open-side. These envelopes are 9 × 12 inches, opening on the 9-inch side. The two types can be used interchangeably, depending on your preference.

Self-Sealing Envelopes are what their name implies. These envelopes are used mainly for interoffice correspondence.

String with Button and Clasp Envelopes are used for interoffice correspondence; both can be sealed and resealed over and over again. These envelopes are not meant to be mailed.

Window Envelopes have a glassine window so that the addressee's name shows through. Thus the person's name and address on correspondence can be used as the mailing address, which avoids duplication of effort, reduces errors, and saves money.

Envelopes can be special. Consider the envelope the introduction to you or your product, and treat it with appropriate care. This way, you're almost sure to make a favorable impression on the recipient.

CHAPTER 16

WRITING AN EFFECTIVE PRINTING BID REQUEST AND PURCHASE ORDER

et's look at what you need if you have to buy printing. You already have the first thing, this book. You also need a PMS swatch book. PMS is "Pantone Matching System." Each color in the swatch book has a number assigned to it. These are like paint chips. PMS colors can fade with age. The yellowing of the paper can also make the colors warmer than they should be. Make sure you always have a fresh book.

The Basics

You will need paper samples. You can get these from area paper merchants. Unless your company has them, you will need to create your own requests for quotations and purchase orders. If you decide that the printing negatives belong to your company, you should make note of this on your RFQ and PO. The Printing Trade Customs say the negatives are the property of the printer. Also, you may wish to include in your RFQ and PO that you will not pay for overruns and you will not accept underruns.

You can describe how you want your client's job packaged and delivered. Purchase orders should be at least two-part forms, so you will have a copy after one is sent to the printer. You will also need a printing RFQ form. The obvious is true. The bigger the project the more complex the RFQ has to be.

Printing Request For Quotation

Design+Associates, Inc.

100 Xenia Drive

Anytown, USA 10000

(212) 555 4444

To: Acme Printing Co., Inc./ John Doe

From: Design+Associates, Inc./ Bill Smith

Re: XYZ Corporation Capabilities Brochure

Date: 8/7/99

This is a request for a quotation for the printing of the XYZ Corporation Capabilities Brochure. Please fax your quote to Jane Smith, Project Director at fax # (212) 555 5555 and mail hard copy.

Size: 8.5" × 11" folded

No. pages: 16 plus cover

Binds: Saddle stitched on the 11" side

Stock: LOE Dull 80lb Cover and LOE Gloss 100lb Text

Quantity: 5,000 Copies

Copy: QuarkXPress 3.2 disk w/ 300 DPI Proofs

Due date: 10/11/99

Deliver to: XYZ Corporation

Invoice: XYZ Corporation

Quote: $ _____

All negatives belong to Design+Associates, Inc. D+A will not pay for overruns and will not accept underruns unless authorized by an officer of the company.

The Purchase Order

The purchase order is the most important document you prepare. It is not only your formal order to the printer, it is your written contract and your instructions as well. I have seen purchase orders make the difference in disputes over thousands of dollars.

If your printing specifications change, I recommend preparing an updated or revised PO with a new date. It's up to you to cover your bases. Yours may be one of hundreds of jobs in the printing plant. It is easier for you to detail your own project, and it's more important to you. It is very important that you set up a job-numbering system. These numbers are your only method of tracking invoices. The PO number is important as it distinguishes what service and vendor you are using, but the job number is your record of the entire project.

Job numbers are very important for tracking. All purchase orders should have that number on them. You can also give each of your clients numbers. These can simply be their phone numbers.

The purchase order is best used if it is introduced at the beginning of a project. You need to establish your own ground rules. Life is one long string of negotiations, and as with most negotiations, there is a closing with a signed agreement. If your purchase order is the only signed agreement, you stand a good chance of prevailing in a dispute, even if the only signature present is your own.

I have talked about purchase orders for printers and the example I have shown is specifically designed for a printing project. Purchase orders are for every purchase. They are the paper trails that are your contracts with all vendors. It's a sloppy world out there, so make sure you are the one in control of your project or purchase, not your vendor. There are two other elements that must appear on an effective purchase order, the price and the due date.

If your company is not buying the printing, instead of having the words "Purchase Order" you can title the form "Start Order."

Purchase Order

Design+Associates, Inc.   PO #1000

100 Xenia Drive   Job #2000
Anytown, USA 10000

(212) 555-4444

To:	Acme Printing Co., Inc.
From:	Design+Associates, Inc.
Re:	XYZ Corporation Capabilities Brochure
Date:	8/7/99

This is a purchase order for the printing of the XYZ Corporation Capabilities Brochure. The job number and purchase order number must appear on all invoices. The specifications are as follows:

Size:	8.5" × 11" folded
Colors:	Two PMS colors with dull spot varnish
No. pgs:	16 plus cover
Binds:	Saddle stitched on the 11" side
Stock:	LOE Dull 80lb Cover and LOE Gloss 100lb Text
Quantity:	5,000 Copies
Copy:	3.2 QuarkXPress disk w/ 300 DPI Proofs

Due date:	10/11/99
Deliver to:	XYZ Corporation
Invoice:	XYZ Corporation
Quote:	$10,000.00

All disks and copy must be returned to Design+Associates, Inc. All negatives belong to D+A. Design+Associates, Inc. will not pay for overruns and will not accept underruns unless authorized by an officer of the company.

_____

For: Design+Associates, Inc.   Date

The purchase order does not have to be a form. It can be a handwritten document. The most important thing is that it is trackable. This means it must have a PO number and a job number on it. You should retain a copy, even if it is a photocopy.

I can't say this too often. This one form may save you a ton of trouble, which translates to money. Don't let any job leave home without it. It could easily be the only document carrying any weight in a legal dispute.

Vendors and Your Purchase Order

It is smart to make sure each vendor is aware of your purchase order system. They should be aware that unless they reference your job number and your purchase order number on each of their invoices, they might not get paid.

If the alteration charges are more than 10 percent of the cost of the initial work, your client is making too many changes.

It is also important for you to issue a new purchase order every time you send a vendor an update (change order). This references those changes so you know what the changes cost your client. If your client's alteration charges are more than 10 percent of the cost of the initial work, your client is making too many changes.

Don't criticize. Suggest that they proof more carefully. After the designer makes the changes, give the page proofs back to the person who gave you the manuscript. They may in turn show it to their boss who will make changes. If they had their boss sign off on the original manuscript, the changes may have been minimal. This is beyond your control and part of their company's politics.

BILLING
FOR YOUR TIME AS A
SALESPERSON

Charging a client for your services goes against the grain of sales. Selling is considered overhead by most companies. But that is not always true, and in this chapter you will learn how to become a valuable consultant to your clients and a profit center for your company. If you are the company, the graphic designer, and the bookkeeper all rolled into one, we'll look at billing methods.

Billing for Your Time

Let's look at what you can bill for. As I mentioned, you can become a profit center for your company if you provide services that your company can bill to your client. Most people in sales never think of these ways of being multifaceted. Your initiative will make you a far more valuable salesperson than other candidates who lack your skills and business savvy.

Consultation/Research

If you are providing consultation specific to the planning of a project, your time should be billable. This is only true if you can provide a "value added" service, not sales chit-chat. A good rule of thumb is to ask the question: Could this process be completed just as successfully and on schedule without my input or assistance? If the answer is "yes," then don't count your time as billable.

If you are doing research to aid a designer, this should be billable. After all, the designer's time performing this same function would be billable. If your company doesn't have a formula for billing your services, you can use various methods to determine your hourly rate. We'll look at methods of doing this a little later in this chapter.

Print Management

This one area can make you an invaluable member of the professional team. If you ask to attend press inspections with a designer, you will learn what to look for and how to mark press sheets.

There are printing plants that will welcome your visit. They will answer any questions you might have without laughing at your lack of knowledge. If you can provide print management, your company should be able to bill for your time. This is a tremendous relief for the harried designer who would prefer to be designing rather than press inspecting. It also makes you worth more than other salespeople because you *can* provide a billable service. Most people miss opportunities by staying within the parameters of their job description. No one has ever achieved greatness only by doing the job they were expected to do.

Writing/Editing

Another obvious but overlooked service that you can provide is writing or editing. This may intimidate you if you are not writing professionally. If you aren't but you want to provide this valuable service, there are courses available from many colleges and universities throughout the country.

Editing is just an extension of writing. Remember the chapter on proofreading. That's part of editing and should be billable. If your company elects not to bill for these services, you will still have developed another facet of your professional value to your company and possibly a potential employer.

Most people don't realize that they are already providing this service internally. If you're writing proposals, letters to clients, or press releases, you are already writing. Why not improve your skills in these areas as well? No one can write too well.

---

*If you're writing
proposals, letters to clients, or press releases,
you are already writing.*

Deliveries

You probably take layouts, proofs, and disks to your client as well as to the printer. Most salespeople charge nothing for this service, but they acknowledge that the client would've paid for a courier. You should make sure that this service is billed to the client at the same rate a courier service would.

This can add up to several hundred dollars a week that could offset your entire expense account. Smart companies bill for everything that is billable. You're not doing a visible favor for your client by not charging for legitimate services.

You may want to develop a simple form for these deliveries. My company is in the Washington, D.C., metropolitan area, and the courier services have divided the area into zones. The delivery charges vary by zone and distance. This a fair way to adjust delivery charges, and once you know the costs, you can design similar rates and apply them to your form. You should fill out the form for each delivery and turn it in to bookkeeping. This is also a good way to keep track of your mileage if you're being reimbursed for it by the company. If this form is to be your mileage record as well as the company's, you may want to design it as a carbonless two-part form so you can keep a copy.

The form on the next page is just one example. You can design your own to suit your needs. The simpler the better. The more complicated the form, the less likely you'll be to fill it out on a day-to-day basis.

Design + Associates, Inc.

Delivery By Hand Form

Date: _____

Client: _____

Job #: _____

To: _____ From: _____

Delivery Charge: $ _____

Mileage (To and From) _____

_____
Signature

What is Your Time Worth?

Your company may not have a formula for billing your time. You can use the system outlined here. First, you must affix an hourly rate to your billable labor. This can be one rate for everyone in your company, or it can be an individual rate for each person. You can use the hourly rates to determine a cost by project.

I've found the most effective way to determine an hourly rate is simply to multiply your actual hourly rate by four. If you're making $30,000 a year, that hourly rate is $15. I use ratios, and in this case, let's use four times your salaried hourly rate. Your billable rate is $15 × 4 = $60 per hour. This takes into consideration your benefits and overhead such as rent, phones, supplies, administrative personnel, and the like. This type of formula is used by lawyers and accountants.

You can vary the ratio depending on where the company is located. Obviously the East and West Coasts are going to be higher, so you might use 4 to 4.5 for New York and 3 to 3.5 for a more rural area.

Since your billable hourly rate is based on your salary, this presupposes that the more you are paid, the more you can bill for your time. Billing by a ratio of your hourly rate should mean that if you are paid more money, you're capable of working faster than someone making less or you perform more valuable tasks.

This ratio or formula is used by lawyers and accountants.

To keep track of your billable time, you need a system. Each project probably has a number already assigned to it. If not, start a numbering system, and use the simplest workable way to assign client and job numbers to individual projects. As mentioned earlier, the client's number could be his or her phone number. This makes it simple to contact them and guarantees that each number will be different.

Next, you should design a time sheet to keep a daily record for each job. I've tried weekly records, but people have a tendency to wait until the end of the week to fill them out. At that point, they are just guessing.

The time sheet on page 131 is very simple but adequate. You could make your codes letter abbreviations for services, like *CM* for client meeting or *R* for research. If your hourly rate in the example is $60, your day's work is worth $480. This is an unrealistic goal for you as a salesperson. Your time managing an account isn't billable unless you perform billable functions.

When the time sheet is turned in, someone must enter the hours and codes into a data bank that will be used to generate an invoice. There are simple programs that can be adapted to run this system. A more sophisticated approach is to network everyone into a central system so that the times and codes are immediately posted to each project electronically.

If you want to reduce the billing-for-hours system to its simplest form, you could average out the time used by individuals to complete a project and apply a total figure based on the size and scope of the job. However, this only works accurately if you have a constant repetition of similar projects. For the most part, it would be nearly useless in a small or large design company. There are pitfalls to any system and the best precaution is paying attention to details.

On the next page, I have created a simple *daily* timesheet. You can code your billable work any way you wish to. I suggest that you also record unbillable work as well, as this becomes a record of the time you have worked.

Time Sheet

Design + Associates, Inc.

Name: Jane Doe
Date: 8/7/00

Job #	Hours	Code
1000	2.5	Writing
1001	.5	Editing
1003	1.0	Client Meeting
1008	.5	Research
1015	.5	Print Management
1001	.25	Print Management
1028	.5	Editing
1014	1.0	Research
1000	.5	Writing
1003	.25	Overhead
1028	.5	Editing
Total	**8.0**	

TERMS AND TRADE CUSTOMS

*Understanding is the key
to communicating.*

BUSINESS TERMS COMMONLY USED IN THE GRAPHIC ARTS

The following terms are meant to help you understand words that may be thrown around while you are negotiating with your client, photographer, printer, or others. You may know most of these words and this might seem silly, but this section may just reaffirm and further clarify what you thought you knew.

Your suppliers have an advantage. They are in business to survive, and the terms they use are precise. They cannot afford misunderstandings or mistakes that could kill their companies. By the same token, you must realize exactly what is being said to you, verbally or in writing. No good businessperson wants to surprise his client at the end of a project with an invoice full of unexpected charges. But it's "buyer beware," and you need to know as much as you can if you're buying illustration, photography, or printing for your client.

The following business terms are presented because they relate directly to you, the seller of graphic arts products and services. In addition, it is important that you have a basic understanding of business in general. If you are selling a service that affects your client's bottom line, you must know more than just the technical terms of the industry. As you know, business is profit. No profit, no client, no design company, and no job for you.

Business Terms

Accounts Payable is the money owed by a company to a creditor for goods or services purchased.

Accounts Receivable is the money owed to a company for work performed and invoices issued. Your invoices are your receivables.

Aging is the money owed to a company, noted by the length of time it has been outstanding. This is measured in 30-, 60-, 90-, or 120-day increments. Aging is very important to banks when considering a loan for a company.

Alterations are changes you make to work completed correctly by your supplier. This is the one area you must try to control because it's probably your company's greatest area of wasted money. The industry average for alteration is said to be 10 percent. Don't believe it. It's really more like 30 to 40 percent.

Arbitration is settling a dispute through an individual or a panel, rather than in a court of law. If both parties can agree on this method, they will save legal fees and court costs.

Blueline is the last proof, and must be considered sacred. The blueline is probably one of the most important documents you'll ever sign. This proof is made from the final negatives that will be used to make the actual printing plates, and that's why blueline corrections are so expensive.

BPA, or "Blanket Purchase Agreement," is an open or standing purchase order for an amount of money you can spend with a supplier. BPAs are used for multiple projects during a given time frame. For instance, a BPA for ninety days for $20,000 to a supplier means you can spend the $20,000 on different projects for ninety days. Every company qualifies service companies differently, so learn about your company's procedures from your accounts payable staff.

BPO, or "Blanket Purchase Order," is the same as a blanket purchase agreement. Some companies use one term, some use the other. It is an open or standing purchase order for an amount of money your company can spend with a supplier.

Brokering is when someone buys a good or service and resells it to another. A service charge is usually added to the cost, and this markup is the broker's profit.

Cash Flow is the coming and going of money that every business experiences. It is the constant cycle of invoicing, being paid, paying out cash to suppliers, and making payroll. Interruptions in cash flow will cause companies to borrow money.

Change Orders, another term for alterations, are changes made to existing work or proofs. They are billable, just like other alterations, and you can control them.

Comp Time is hours given as time off for hours worked as overtime. Companies paying comp time should not bill more than their normal hourly rate for overtime situations. This is a practice of accountants.

Contract is a written agreement between two parties outlining the responsibilities of each. A contract can be no more than a memo from one party to the next, spelling out the terms of the agreement. If the recipient does not respond, then the party sending the memo is presumed to be correct. You can create your own "paper trail" and protect yourself from liabilities that your supplier assumes you will accept. This is important because, in our society, virtually all business is conducted on the basis of contract.

Cost Per M is cost per thousand. When asking for a printing estimate or quotation over five thousand copies, it pays to ask for a price for additional thousands at the time of the initial run.

Estimate is a best-guess calculation of what a good or service will cost. An estimate is not necessarily a bottom-line cost. It is not a quotation or a formal proposal.

FOB means "Freight on Board." This term is used to specify location of delivery, such as FOB Detroit.

Indemnification is protection from legal reprisal. If you agree to someone's indemnification in a situation, you are agreeing that they are not liable in that situation. In addition, there are certain situations where an individual is automatically indemnified. For instance, if a graphic designer designs a logo for your company and another designer creates the same logo at the same time for another company, your designer is not liable for any lawsuits stemming from that design because your designer was acting on good faith and unknowingly created the same logo. Your best protection is to start the registration process as soon as possible.

Invoice is a bill for a specific product or service, and only one invoice is issued. Most companies pay invoices only, never statements. Unpaid invoices will appear on monthly statements, and interest may be charged against the unpaid balance. If you have a dispute over an invoice, you should pay immediately any portion not in dispute. Any dispute should be called to the seller's attention prior to the invoice becoming past due.

Letter of Intent is a letter defining the terms of an agreement. It can be from a supplier to you, or from you to a supplier. When there is no contract, this is the next best thing. And if you generate the letter, you can make sure you are fully protected. Always respond to a letter of intent in writing if the letter to you is not correct. A verbal response can easily be forgotten at a crucial later date.

Liability in business means exposure to legal action or financial responsibility. It is up to you to understand each facet of the graphic arts process affecting you. Ignorance is not protection, and every letter, memo, or other written document decreases your liability. You can transfer liability in the beginning, but when it's too late, you can be hung with it. Always create your own insurance with a paper trail.

Markup is a handling charge. Markups can be any amount added to a good or service bought by a supplier for you. Usually markups do not include any service by a designer or broker. You can save money by having a supplier, such as a printer, bill you direct.

Out-of-Pocket Expenses are costs to your designer, photographer, or printer in addition to their labor. Other consultants will often give these suppliers a flat fee for their services plus out-of-pocket expenses. This can be tricky, so get a written definition of

138

what "out-of-pocket expenses" really means. For instance, you don't want to buy someone a car so he can travel on your behalf!

PEs are "Printer's Errors," or errors made by your supplier. They are often noted as PEs so that you won't be charged for them. However, if there are just a few PEs and many changes made by your company, it will be very hard for the supplier to delineate or separate his PEs from your alterations.

Photo Art Direction is the time a designer spends supervising photography and reviewing proofs. Here again, it is better to have the photography billed directly to you and for the designer only to bill you for the time he or she is needed to perform art direction.

Print Management is the time a designer spends working with a printer. Creating a schedule, providing specifications, checking proofs, and press inspecting are all part of print management.

Printing Overrun is when a printer runs more copies than you have ordered. Check with the printer as to your liability in such an instance because some printers will charge for the excess. Make sure you understand the printer's terms and conditions. You do have the opportunity to dictate your own terms, specifically that you will not pay for overage, in your purchase order.

Printing Underrun is a run that is short. The printer may say in their terms and conditions of sale that a percentage of underage is acceptable. Here again, as the client, you can disagree in your purchase order.

Proposal is a fixed-price bid for a good or service. Usually proposals will contain: a capability statement showing the supplier's credentials, a project overview, a technical proposal stating how the supplier intends to accomplish the project goals, a cost proposal, résumés of key individuals who will work on the project, and references with phone numbers.

Registered Trademark is a logo or logotype that has been registered through the U.S. Patent and Trademark Office. An *R* in a circle (®) signifies that the trademark has been registered. If you are in a position within your company to recommend registering your company's logo, I strongly urge you to do so. Remember indemnification; the first company to initiate registration has the best chance of the design's survival as their own property.

RFP is a "Request for Proposal." This is usually a form sent to suppliers, inviting them to submit a proposal on a specific project. Be sure to note on the RFP that it is not a purchase order. Make sure your specifications and project goals are clear. Don't use ambiguous language.

RFQ is a "Request for Quotation," and is the same as an RFP.

Search is the work you perform prior to submitting a logo or logotype for formal registration. The U.S. Patent and Trademark Office will help you if you wish to try to do this yourself, but my advice is to let a lawyer take this step.

Servicemark is used when the logo or logotype represents a service rather than a product. This is indicated by a small *SM* next to the mark.

Spec Work is work performed in speculation of receiving a project and is done when several graphic designers are asked to submit free designs with their proposal. The American Institute of Graphic Arts and the Graphic Design Trade Customs are strictly against this practice, and the majority of designers will refuse to do spec work. Companies who want multiple design choices will often offer a fee to several design firms, but design contests other than for charity are considered speculative.

Statement is a summary of your company's account with a supplier. A statement shows your outstanding balance, often by thirty-day aging stages. It is not an invoice, but it will list invoices already sent to you.

Terms are the number of days after which a supplier expects full payment for goods or services. Thirty days is usually the length of the term. Interest may be charged after thirty days, in the same way a credit card company would charge your personal account.

Thirty Days Net means complete payment in thirty days. It does not mean installment payments or other extended terms.

Trademark is the term used when the logo or logotype represents a product, not a service. This is shown by a small *TM* next to the mark.

Transmittal Letter or Letter of Transmittal is a note or letter stating something has been sent from one company to another. If it is a package coming to you, the transmittal letter will tell you what you should be getting, and the sender will retain a copy of the letter for their protection. This is an excellent device for you to use as well.

CHAPTER 19

COMMONLY USED
GRAPHIC ARTS AND
COMPUTER TERMS

The following terms and definitions have been compiled to aid you in communicating with other graphic arts professionals. These definitions have been updated to include terms used in electronic design, prepress, and printing.

To list all of the terms used in the field of graphic arts would be counterproductive. Many are either too technical or have little meaning in your areas of responsibility. These are basic terms which are necessary for memos, proposals, RFQs, BPOs, purchase orders, and contracts.

Graphics Terms

AAs are "Author's Alterations." These are changes made to the copy by the author and are considered billable to you the client.

Absorption is the rate at which paper takes liquid such as ink. It is also the rate at which light is transmitted through a translucent surface.

Accordion Fold is used to describe a brochure, pamphlet, etc., with two or more parallel folds resulting in an accordion-like format.

Additive Color is the term used when describing the combination of the pure colors of red, green, and blue. When combined electronically they produce white, or are totally transparent. RGB is the acronym for these colors and generally refers to transmitted color, such as that seen on a computer monitor or television screen.

Against the Grain describes paper that is folded at a ninety degree angle to the direction of its grain. This is usually considered the least acceptable way to fold a sheet because it often causes cracking.

Airbrush is a way of applying color with a spray. It also defines an effect simulated electronically to give something a soft edge or a gradation of tone.

Analog Color is color that is transmitted in a nondigital manner. In printing, it refers to a color proof pulled from conventional separations.

Antique Finish is a natural rough finish of certain printing papers.

Aperture is the opening of a camera lens. The f-stop number signifies the size of the lens opening.

Art or **Artwork** refers to a mechanical or components of a mechanical to be photographed for the creation of a negative for printing. The new electronic technology refers to a prepress disk as a mechanical.

Ascender is the part of a lowercase letter that is raised in a line of type, such as the back of an *h*.

Backbone is the back spine of a hard-bound or perfect-bound book.

Backing Up is the printing of the reverse side of a sheet.

Bad Break in typography is any line that ends with a widow or begins with an orphan. (See Widow and Orphan definitions.)

Basis Weight is the weight in pounds of five hundred sheets of paper in a standard size for a printing press. Five hundred sheets of a printing paper that measures 25 × 38 inches of 60 pound text has a basis weight of sixty pounds.

Bit, in computer terminology, is a single unit of numerical information. The word is derived from BI*nary digi*T.

Bit Map, in computer terminology, is the complete image or page with all information portrayed by pixels.

Black Printer is the black in four-color printing. It is the *K* in CMYK (cyan-magenta-yellow-black) notations.

Blanket is the rubber-surfaced roller on an offset press that receives the ink from the printing plate and transfers it to paper.

Bleed is when an image, photograph, or area of color seems to run off the edge of a printed page.

Blind Embossing is the printing process where an image is raised on a sheet of paper through the use of dies, without color.

Blueline is a proof made with photosensitized paper from the final offset negatives that will be used to make the final printing plates. The color of the exposed area is blue.

Body Copy is the main portion of text in a printed piece. This is in contrast to "Heads" and "Subheads."

Boldface is the term used to describe type heavier in weight than the normal strength of its text face.

Bond is a grade of writing paper used for letters and forms, which generally comes in a 17×22–inch sheet size.

Book Paper may be coated or uncoated and usually comes in a 25×38–inch sheet.

Break for Color is the keying of elements and areas for their assigned colors in printing. These can be screens, solids, or process builds. These are also called "color breaks."

Brochure is generally any printed promotional piece that is more than two pages. A brochure can be a simple as a 4-panel, 4×9–

inch pamphlet or an elaborate 64-page, 8.5 × 11–inch, full-color corporate capabilities promotion. Generally a two page (front and back) promotion is considered a "flyer."

Bulk refers to thickness of paper. This is often used in book printing to give the desired thickness to the final printed product.

Burn is the term used when a printing negative is placed on photosensitized paper or a printing plate, and is exposed to light to form a proof or a printing plate.

Byte is a single unit of digital information within a computerized image.

CAD-CAM is "Computer Assisted Design" and "Computer Assisted Manufacturing."

Calender is the process that gives smoothness and gloss to a sheet of paper at the end of the papermaking process.

Caliper is the thickness of paper, usually measured in the thousandths of an inch, called "mils."

Camera-ready Art (CRA) means that copy is ready to be photographed to make negatives for offset printing.

Caps are capital letters. Hence, "all caps" means all capital letters.

Cast Coated is a paper that has been coated so that ink will stand up on the surface and offer the best representation of color. Most paper companies keep their coating processes secret.

CD-ROM stands for "Compact Disk—Read Only Memory." The CD is just like your stereo CD, but works with graphic images instead of just music. ROM means you can read the information on the disk, but you can't record on it.

Character is one letter or a symbol in a typeface.

CMYK is Cyan, Magenta, Yellow and *K* for Black. These are the ink colors used in four-color process printing. They are subtractive colors, as all four combined make black.

Coated Paper is paper that has received a coating of some kind in the manufacturing stage. These papers can be made in any color and can be dull or glossy. Ink generally stands up extremely well on this type of paper, which makes these papers a favorite among graphic designers.

Collate is the arrangement of multiple sheets or pages in their correct order.

Color Balance is the correct relationship of four process colors.

Color Correction is any method used to correct an imbalance of color in a printed image. Formerly, dot-etching was often used to change the structure of a color subject by hand-altering the density or number of dots in a given area. Now color corrections can be made electronically on the computer.

Color Keys are clear color overlays (usually made by 3M) to proof color breaks.

Color Proofs are representations of any color images or full-color images that let you see the effect of the colors that have been specified.

Color Separation is the division of each of the four process colors into their respective percentages that make up a full-color image or picture.

Condensed Type is a compressed letterform that occupies less area than the normal letterforms.

Contacts are photographic prints made by negatives directly exposed to photosensitized paper.

Continuous Tone is a photograph that has no dot structure. This is the opposite of a halftone.

Copy is material furnished by you to a graphic designer or a printer and may include illustrations as well as text.

Cromalin is a color proof using the DuPont Cromalin process.

Crop is the term used to size and shape photographs or illustrations for reproduction.

CRT is a Cathode Ray Tube on a computer monitor, which is the monochromatic (one-color) or full-color video display.

Curl is the effect on paper caused by the differences of coatings from one side to the other.

Cut-off is the print length of a sheet of paper on a web press or a paper machine.

Cyan is process blue, one of the four basic colors in four-color process printing.

Dandy Roll is a cylinder that creates a watermark in a sheet of paper during the papermaking process.

Deckle Edge is the edge of a sheet of paper that has been created to look torn or ragged. This effect is used on formal invitations and specialty printing projects.

Densitometer is an instrument that measures the density of printing ink on paper.

Descender is the part of a lowercase letter that extends below the the rest of the characters such as the back of a lowercase letter *p*. This is the opposite of an ascender.

Die Cutting is a process by which a shape is cut through a piece of paper by using a die. A die resembles a sharp cookie cutter and can be used to create special folders or shapes.

Digital Color Proofs are proofs produced from electronic data. Conventional proofs need film, whereas digital proofs utilize digital information generated from a computer.

Digital Plates are generated without negatives directly from an electronic prepress system.

Digital Printing is plateless printing through electronic prepress. The process is very effective for on-demand four-color printing.

Dimensional Stability is the ability of paper or film to maintain its size and shape during changes in the moisture content and humidity within its environment.

Display Type is type used for headlines. It is generally used for titles and it is set larger than other text within in the same area.

Dot is the smallest area of density in a halftone. If you look at any printed black-and-white picture with a magnifying glass (preferably in a newspaper because the screen is so coarse), you will see the dots that make up the picture.

Dot Etching is a way of altering a four-color image by using chemicals to eliminate or increase dots on the negatives or positives for any of the color in certain areas.

Dot Gain occurs when the dots in printing become larger and cause the ink to reproduce darker or more intensely than it should.

Dots per Inch (DPI) is the measure of how many electronic dots per inch are generated by a computer-linked printer. The more dots per inch, the sharper and crisper the image will be.

Draw Down is the process of spreading ink on a sheet of paper by hand with a spatula to test color.

Dummy is a bound replica of a planned printed piece. A dummy can be just a folded and stapled sample made up of plain paper, or it can be a complete bound proof.

Duotone is a process of giving a black-and-white photograph a two-color look. Consult your printer on the various duotone effects available. There is also a Pantone Matching System book showing duotones available in art supply stores.

Duplex Stock is paper that has two different sheets laminated together so that a different color or finish is on each side.

Dye Transfer is a photographic process for intensifying color and retouching photographs through the use of dyes. This process has been replaced by electronic retouching.

Electronic Dot Generation (EDG) is the method for creating halftones electronically.

Em is a measurement in typography representing the space and size an *M* occupies in each font.

Emulsion Side is the treated side of film that collects light causing a photographic image to appear.

En is a measurement in typography representing roughly the space an *N* occupies, or half an em space.

Enamel is the term used for the coating on certain gloss papers.

EPS (Encapsulated PostScript File) is a picture file format that allows PostScript information to be transferred between computer systems. EPS files are limited in the way they can be manipulated. The image can be scaled in both black-and-white and color.

Expanded Type is a typeface that is set wider than the normal version was designed.

Felt Side is the smoother side of a sheet of paper. It is generally the top of the sheet when it's being manufactured.

Flat is composite film that is ready to be converted into an offset printing plate through exposure to light.

Flatbed Scanner is a four-color scanner that scans an image flat, in contrast to wrapping the original around a drum.

Flush Left, Ragged Right is the term for type that is not justified on the right side.

Folio is a page number either at the top or bottom of a page.

Font is a specific typeface or type style.

Fountain is the area that adds water or synthetic gum to one of the printing cylinders on a printing press.

Front-end System, in electronic prepress, is the desktop area in the production and printing process.

Galley Proof is running type before it is made into pages. Galleys are usually associated with older typesetting methods or book production. Computerized design systems bypass this stage and give the reader complete pages.

Gathering, in print binding, is the assembly of folded signatures in their correct sequence.

GCR is the "Gray Component Replacement."

Generation is each stage beyond the original in the reproduction process of an image, either text or illustrative materials.

Gigabyte (GB) is one billion bytes.

Grain is the direction of the fibers within a sheet of paper. Folding against the grain can cause cracking. Grain "long" or "short" means which way the grain is running in a sheet.

Grayscale is the range of gray measured from white to black. Color density can also be measured by a grayscale.

Gripper is the part of a printing press that holds and moves a sheet of paper.

Gumming is part of the plate-making process. Gum is applied to the areas on a printing plate that will not take ink.

Gutter is the inner margin of a bound publication.

Hairline is the thinnest rule possible that will hold up in the printing process.

Halftone is the reproduction of a continuous-tone image screened so that dots are formed, and the image can be printed.

Hardcopy is any visual material that is not on a computer screen, such as a manuscript, laser proof, or photocopy.

Hardware is the physical computer equipment, as opposed to software, which is information that operates the equipment.

Hickeys are spots where ink does not adhere to the paper surface during the printing process.

Highlight is the lightest area in a halftone, containing the fewest dots.

Holdout is the property within a sheet of paper which lets the ink set up and gives the richest color. Too much holdout can cause problems when one sheet's ink rubs off on another. This is called "off-setting."

HSV is "Hue, Saturation, and Value." This describes the luminance in computer graphic programs.

Hue is pure color, versus a tint or a shade. Tints of color have white added to them. Shades of color have black added to them.

Imagesetter is a device used to output paper or film from electronically generated information.

Imposition is the order or position of pages on a printing form that will make up the correct signatures when trimmed.

Impression, in printing, is the term for each time the printing press comes in contact with a sheet of paper.

Insert is a sheet of paper, blown in or bound into a publication.

Italic is type that is designed to slant right.

Justify, in typography, is text that is both flush left and flush right. This book's text is justified.

152

Kerning, in typography, is the decreasing or increasing of the space between the individual letters in copy.

Keyboard is the unit containing keys on a computer. To *keyboard* copy is to type text into the computer.

Keyline is an outline indicating color breaks and other information for the prepress process.

Kiss Impression is the lightest impression possible to leave an image in the printing process.

Kraft is paper or board made from unbleached pulp, usually tan.

Laid Paper is made with a pattern of parallel lines in the sheets, such as a ribbed effect. These papers have a specific personality and are used to achieve a specific look.

Lamination is a process in which heat is used to apply a plastic film to a printed sheet of paper. This coating can be applied with a liquid ("liquid lamination") and makes the sheet more durable and colors appear more vivid.

Laser stands for "Light Amplification by Stimulated Emission of Radiation." In prepress, lasers are used to produce images from digital data.

Layout is a graphic design term used for a prototype showing color and typographical relationships. In printing, a layout is the format of the pages.

Leaders are the dots in horizontal rows, as in tabular materials. Leaders draw the eye across the page, as in a table of contents.

Leading in typesetting is the space between lines of text.

Letterspacing is the increase of the space between letters.

Line Copy is copy that does not need a screen to be reproduced. A line drawing is an illustration that is made up of black and white areas only.

Local Area Network (LAN) is the linking of computer equipment. In the prepress area, it is the connecting of workstations and other peripheral equipment such as scanners and printers.

Logo or Logotype is the symbol or stylized word designed to identify an organization, product, or service. Logos are the symbols. Logotypes are the stylized words or names. A company can have a logo and logotype such as "Johnson's Wax." That company uses a stylized *J* for its logo and spells out its name in a unique typestyle as its logotype.

Lowercase is the opposite of capital letters or "caps." The word "case" comes from the compartmented wooden boxes in which these letters were stored when type was set by hand. "Commoncase" is type that is designed to use upper- and lowercase letters in the same sizes and weights.

M is the abbreviation for one thousand in the measurement of paper quantities or printed copies.

Magenta is process red. The color is a pinkish hue, and does not look like traditional red.

Make Ready is the process of setting up a printing press for a run. Inferior sheets are run through the press to get the color balanced. These are called "make-ready sheets."

Matte Finish in paper means a dull surface.

Measure is the width of a line of text in typesetting, usually calculated in picas.

Megabyte (MB) is the term for one million bytes. Disk capacity and RAM are usually measured in megabytes.

Menu is the computer term for choices of functions offered on the computer monitor.

Modem (MO*dulator*/DEM*odulator*) is equipment used to send

154

information over phone lines from one electronic system to another. It converts data into high-frequency signals.

Moiré is an undesirable pattern created when screen angles are incorrect. The pattern often appears as a plaid.

Monitor is a computer video screen.

Mouse is a device that lets the computer operator move the cursor around on the screen by sliding a handheld unit over a pad.

Mylar is a polyester film used in stripping. It has great strength and is very stable.

Negative is a piece of film with reversed images produced from a conventional camera or an imagesetter, and is used to produce a printing plate.

Newsprint is the type of paper used in the printing of newspapers. Made from ground wood pulp, it is inexpensive when compared to most grades of commercial printing papers.

Oblong is the term used for a booklet or publication bound on the shorter side.

OCR is "Optical Character Reader." As the name implies, OCR converts/reads written or printed text and turns it into digital information for the computer.

Off-loading, or removal of data from a computer, is performed when more memory is needed. This is also called "downloading."

Offset is the lithographic printing process, whose name derives from the fact that the offset printing plate never touches the paper. An intermediate roller or blanket receives the image from the plate and transfers it to the paper.

Opacity is the opposite of transparency or translucency. It is the quality of paper to hide show-through so that you don't see the images on the other side of the sheet.

Opaque is the process of covering areas on an offset negative to prevent exposure in nonprint areas.

Orphan is a single line of type beginning or ending a paragraph that is at the bottom or top of the page.

Overlay is usually a transparent material covering mechanical artwork used for marking corrections, color breaks, or variable print runs.

Overrun is the number of copies printed in excess of the number ordered. Underrun, or shortage of copies, is the opposite.

Overset is the amount of text in excess of the space allotted for it.

Page is one side of one half of a sheet of paper in a printed piece. If you pull the center out of a saddle-stitched magazine, you will be holding four pages.

Page Makeup is the assembly of all of the elements that represent a page. These elements can be illustrations, photographs, charts, graphs, typography, etc.

Palette is a group of colors available in a given medium.

Paste-up is the preparing of a conventional mechanical. The term comes from the era when rubber cement was used to literally glue type and other elements down on illustration board. Even with the advent of waxers, these mechanicals were still referred to as paste-ups.

Perfecting Press prints both sides of a sheet of paper with one pass through the printing press.

Phototypesetting is type set through photography. This is also known as "cold type," in contrast to linotype, called "hot type."

Pica is a printing measurement representing approximately one sixth of an inch. The pica measurements are used extensively in typesetting and page geometry.

Picking is the lifting of the printing paper's surface due to the tack of the ink. This occurs when the tack of the ink is stronger than the surface of the sheet.

Pin Register is the use of pegs/pins to align film, negatives, plates, and the like for perfect registration.

Plate is the name of the material carrying the image to be printed, which is loaded onto the press. Plates can be paper, plastic, metal, or other materials.

Point is a printer's measurement. There are twelve points in a pica, or seventy-two points in an inch. The height of type is always measured in points.

Positive is the opposite of a negative. The light and dark areas are the same as the original copy.

PostScript is a computer language connecting different programs as well as platforms.

Press Proof is a proof pulled from running a color subject on a full-color press. This is an expensive way to proof a job, but the new electronic proofing systems are making press proofs less and less necessary.

Process Colors are the four colors used to achieve full-color printing. They're cyan, magenta, yellow, and black (CMYK). These colors are subtractive; when printed full strength over one another, they form black.

Progressive Proofs are made from the process color builds and show the sequence they will run when on press.

Ragged Left or **Rag Left** is the term used to describe type that is not justified on the left side.

Ragged Right or **Rag Right** is the term used to describe type that is not justified on the right side.

Raster Image Processor (RIP) is the processor that reads and converts copy into digital data to be utilized as graphics in a computer system. The term "ripping" is used in describing this process.

Ream is five hundred sheets of paper.

Reflective Copy is any copy to be photographed that isn't transparent. Reflective copy can be scanned into a computer without being photographed.

Registration is the matching of images to make up a perfect unit. Registration marks are guides used to correctly place one element over another.

Resolution is the measurement, in dots per inch (dpi), of paper or film output. The more dots per inch, the better the resolution, and the sharper the output. While 300 dpi is considered low resolution, 1,200 dpi generally represents the beginning of reproduction-quality resolution.

RGB is "Red, Green, and Blue," the main colors utilized by video/computer monitors. These are additive colors. When they are combined in their full values, white is the result. This is the opposite of process colors, which form black when combined in full strength.

Run-around is a term describing type that literally runs around a picture, illustration, or other design element.

Running Head is a headline or title at the top of each page in a publication.

Saddle Stitched is the wire binding method of stitching a booklet. The booklet/publication literally straddles a wire like a saddle and is stapled to hold it together. This is the opposite of perfect bound, where the pages are glued into the booklet and there is a spine.

Scaling is the enlargement or reduction of a graphic element to fit in a specific area.

Scanner is an electronic device that turns a graphic image into digital information to be manipulated by a computer.

Score is to make an impression in a sheet of paper so that cracking when folding is minimized.

Screen is a printing term describing the maximum number of dots in one square inch. A 65-line screen is recommended for newspaper reproduction because it is coarse and will work better with the high absorbency of newsprint. A 200-line screen should only be used with a fine printing paper. The normal screen used by most commercial printers is a 175-line screen.

SCSI (pronounced "scuzzie") means "Small Computer System Interface." SCSI ports are connecting points on a computer for peripherals.

Self Cover means that the paper used for the cover of a pamphlet/publication is the same stock as the text. The opposite is **Plus Cover**, which signifies that the cover stock is different from the text stock.

Serif is the term used for typefaces with thick and thin strokes. The serifs are thin lines, or "feet" appearing at the tops and bottoms of letters. The opposite of serif type is sans serif (or lack of serif). The typeface used here is serif.

Sheetwise means running one side of a sheet of paper through a press, then turning it over and running the other side.

Show-through is the opposite of opaque. This is when the images on the reverse side of a sheet can be seen through it, which is usually undesirable.

Signature is the term describing a printed sheet when it has been folded. Signatures are normally sixteen pages because eight pages can be printed on one side of a 25 × 38–inch sheet.

Silhouette is when a graphic element has had its background removed and appears to float on the page.

Skid is a wooden platform or palette holding paper or printed pages. Skids are used because they hold large quantities and can be easily moved by a forklift.

Small Caps are capital letters that are no higher than the main body of a lower case letter (SMALL CAPS).

Spiral Binding can be wire or plastic, and is a spiral.

Step and Repeat is the process of duplicating pages.

Stet means disregard the changes indicated. This proofreading term is used when the proofreader decides something marked should return to its original state.

Stripping is the positioning of offset negatives for use in creating a plate, as done on conventional prepress.

Surprint means overprint. An example is a yellow box with black type surprinting over it.

Tagged Image File Format (TIFF) is the method for exchanging scanned images between applications.

Text is the body copy within a document, versus the headlines or subheads.

Thermal Printers produce color proofs, using a transfer sheet and heat to transfer images onto a page.

Tints are screen percentages of a solid color.

Tooth is a term used to describe the rough finish of a paper.

Varnish is used to enhance a printed image. Gloss varnish will brighten an image, while a dull varnish will mute it. Varnish is also used to make dark ink less likely to show fingerprints. Special effects can be achieved when tints of ink are added to a varnish. If you are going to flood varnish a solid, however, the paper you use will lose its identity.

Washup is the cleaning of the rollers, fountains, and other parts of a printing press in preparation for the next run. There is a charge for a washup if it's necessary between runs of the same job.

Waterless Printing uses silicone coatings on the plates instead of water. This type of offset printing is environmentally friendly, as it doesn't produce pollution.

Web Press is a printing press that prints from rolls of paper rather than from sheets. Webs are used for long runs, providing economies of time and money for catalogs and other commercial publications.

Widow in typography is one hanging word, or partial word, at the end of a paragraph. This is considered undesirable by many, and you may want to rewrite the paragraph to delete the widow.

Wire-O-Binding is the same as spiral binding, but uses wire instead of plastic.

Wire side of a sheet of paper is the side opposite the felt side. The wire side is not as smooth as the felt side.

Work and Turn is the method of printing one side of a sheet and then turning it over from left to right and using the same plate to print the other side. This is ideal for short forms because there is no washup between the printing of the two sides of the sheet.

WYSIWYG (pronounced "wizzie-wig") means "What You See Is What You Get." This applies to images on a computer monitor. Basically, what the screen shows is what the printer will output.

CHAPTER 20

COMMONLY USED
INTERNET TERMS

The following Internet-related terms and definitions have been compiled to aid you in communicating with clients and graphic arts professionals. These are not all of the definitions, but merely a sampling to get you started.

The terms used to describe Internet services, network technologies, and specific computer programs make little or no sense to a beginner. Internet terminology combines terms from computer networking, business, government, and commercial products. This glossary avoids terms that have been defined by commercial companies for their products.

Internet Terms

10Base-T is a wiring pattern for an Ethernet LAN. The *T* abbreviates twisted pair, the kind of wire connecting a computer to the network.

ACK is the abbreviation for "Acknowledgement."

Address is the number assigned to a computer much like a telephone number is assigned to a home. When data travels from one computer to another, the data contains the numbers assigned to both the sender's and receiver's computers.

Advanced Networks and Services (ANS) is a major Wide Area Network in the Internet which a private company usually owns and operates.

Analog-to-Digital Converter (A-to-D converter) is a converter that turns an analog electrical signal into a sequence of numbers.

Anonymous FTP is a special login "anonymous" to obtain access to public files through the FTP service.

ANSNET is a major Wide Area Network that is part of the Internet. Advanced Networks and Services owns ANSNET.

Applet is a miniature software application, often associated with Web browsers.

Archie is a search service available on the Internet that searches for all files with the same name. The name "archie" is short for archive.

ASCII (Pronounced "Askee") is the "American Standard Code for Information Interchange." This is a general standard for information processed as text characters, usually electronically.

ATM is the abbreviation for "Asynchronous Transfer Mode."

A-to-D converter is an "Analog-to-Digital" converter.

Automated Search Service is a service that locates information without the user making decisions or selecting from menus. Automated search services either search titles or complete documents. Examples include Lycos, Yahoo!, and AltaVista.

Bandwidth is the capacity of a network, usually measured in bits per second. Systems need higher bandwidth for audio or video than for e-mail or other services.

Baud is the number of times per second a signal can change on a transmission line. The baud rate equals the number of bits per second that can be transferred.

Binary Digit (bit) 0 or 1. The Internet uses binary digits to represent information, including: audio, video, and text.

BITNET (*Because It's Time NETwork*) is a network developed at

City University of New York. BITNET lets users exchange e-mail and files, but does not provide other Internet services.

Bits per Second (bps) is the measure of the rate of data transmission. The measure refers to the capacity of a network (see bandwidth).

Bookmark is part of the browser that records a location so it is easy to return to it.

BPS is the abbreviation for "Bits Per Second."

Broadcast is information given to a group of interconnected computers simultaneously.

Browser is a program that lets users view hypermedia documents on the Internet. Netscape Communications and Microsoft Corporation offer two popular browsers.

Browsing is looking for information by repeatedly scanning and selecting information. An Internet browsing service offers a list of items or a menu page of information. The user reads the information, selects an item, and then the service retrieves new information.

BTW is the abbreviation for "By The Way" used in electronic communication.

Bulletin Board Service (BBS) is a service that lets an individual post a message for others to read.

Carrier is an electrical signal used by a modem to encode information for transmission across a telephone connection.

CC (Carbon copy) is a term used in e-mail headers for additional recipients.

CGI is the abbreviation for **Common Gateway Interface**.

Client is a program that contacts a remote server by the Internet. A separate client program is usually needed for each Internet service.

Client-Server Computing are two programs communicating across a network. The requesting program is called the client; the program answering is the server.

Collapsed Backbone is a router used instead of a backbone Local Area Network and connected routers. A collapsed backbone is used because it costs less than the traditional design.

Common Gateway Interface (CGI) uses a computer program to assemble a Web page whenever the user requests the page. Pages composed using CGI technology are not stored on the server's disk before requests arrive.

CompuServe is an organization offering network services through telephone connections. CompuServe subscribers can send and receive e-mail with any user who has a computer on the Internet.

Connection are two programs communicating using **TCP**; the TCP software on the two computers forms a connection across the Internet.

Datagram is the synonym for **IP Datagram**.

Demodulation is the extracting of information from a modulated signal arriving over a telephone line. Demodulation occurs in a modem. (Also see **Modulation** and **Carrier**.)

Destination Address is the numerical value that specifies the computer to which the information has been sent. The destination address is the **IP address** of the destination computer.

Digital Library Information is information that has been stored in digital form. A digital library can include documents, images, sounds, and information gathered from ongoing events.

Digital Technology uses numbers to represent information. A computer is digital because it represents keystrokes, pictures, text, and sounds using numbers.

DNS is the abbreviation for "Domain Name System."

Domain Name is the name assigned to a computer on the Internet. Domain names often end in .com or .edu or .gov.

Dotted Decimal is used to specify an **IP address**. Dotted decimal represents an address as four small, decimal integers separated by periods. A computer stores each IP address in binary dotted decimal notation making addresses easier to enter or read.

E-mail is the abbreviation for "Electronic Mail."

E-mail Address is an address assigned to an electronic mailbox. To send e-mail, enter the e-mail address of the recipient. On the Internet, e-mail addresses usually have the form *person@computer.*

E-mail Alias is shorthand for an e-mail address used to send electronic mail without typing a long e-mail address.

Ethernet is a popular Local Area Network technology invented by the Xerox Corporation. An Ethernet consists of a cable to which computers are attached.

FAQ (Frequently Asked Questions) contains questions most frequently asked and their answers.

File Server Program runs on a computer providing access to files on that computer. The term is often used to describe computers that run file server programs.

File Transfer Protocol (FTP) is the Internet service used to transfer a copy of a file from one computer to another.

Finger is an Internet service used to find out which users are currently logged into a particular computer.

Flame is a term used in electronic communication to mean an emotional or inflammatory note, often written in response to another message. The word is sometimes used as a verb, meaning to write an inflammatory message.

Folder is a synonym for directory.

Frames is a technology that divides a Web page into different areas (i.e., windows), and allows each area to change independently of the others.

FTP is the abbreviation for "File Transfer Protocol."

FYA is the abreviation for "For Your Amusement" used in electronic communication.

Gopher is an Internet browsing service. All information is organized into a hierarchy of menus. Gopher displays a menu on the screen to select an item for a file of information or to another menu.

Home Page is a page of information accessible through the Worldwide Web. The page can contain a mixture of graphics and text, and can include embedded references to other pages. Usually each user and each organization has a separate home page.

Hop Count is a measure of distance in a fileswitching network. If a file must travel through *n* additional routers on its trip from its source to its target, the target is said to lie *n* hops away from the source.

Host is a synonym for user's computer. Each computer is connected to the Internet and is classified as a host or a router.

Hostname is the name assigned to a computer. (See **Domain Name**.)

HTML is the acronym for HyperText Markup Language. This is the computer language used to specify the contents and format of a hypermedia document in the World Wide Web.

HTTP is the acronym for "HyperText Transport Protocol." The protocol used to access a Worldwide Web document. A user may encounter the term HTTP in a **Uniform Resource Locator**.

Hub is an electronic device that connects to several computers and replaces a LAN, usually an Ethernet. Hubs are used with **10Base-T**.

Hypermedia is an information storage system in which each page of information can contain embedded references to images, sounds, and other pages of information.

Hypertext is a system for storing pages of textual information that each contains embedded references to other pages of information. This lets the visitor to a site progress from page to page of information.

IAB is the abbreviation for "Internet Architecture Board."

IETF is the abbreviation for "Internet Engineering Task Force."

IMHO is the abbreviation for "In My Humble Opinion" used in electronic communication.

Information Superhighway is a term used by the public to refer to the national information infrastructure in the United States. The Internet is part of the information infrastructure, which is sometimes called the information highway.

Integrated Circuit is a small, electronic device containing transistors. An integrated circuit is called a chip.

Internet is the collection of networks and routers that use the TCP/IP protocol suite and function as a single, large network.

Internet address is a number. Each computer on the Internet is assigned an **IP address**. Software uses the address to identify the intended recipient when it sends a message. An Internet address is also called an IP address.

Internet Relay Chat (IRC) is a service that lets groups communicate using a keyboard. A group of users creates a channel and sends messages to it and then each active participant for a given channel receives a copy of each message.

Internet Society is a nonprofit organization established to encourage exploration of the Internet.

Internetworking is a term used to refer to planning, building, testing, and using Internet systems.

InterNIC (Internet Network Information Center) is an organization that supplies information about the Internet as well as organizations that provide Internet connectivity.

IP (Internet Protocol) is a specification or the format of files computers use when communicating across the Internet. In practice, the term usually refers to the IP software.

IP Address is a synonym for Internet address.

IP Datagram is a file of data sent across the Internet. The IP file contains the address of the sender, the IP address of the destination, and the information being sent.

IPng is the abbreviation for "Internet Protocol: the Next Generation."

IRC is the abbreviation for "Internet Relay Chat."

ISP (Internet Service Provider) is a company that offers connectivity to the Internet. Telephone and cable television companies, as well as many small, private ISPs, offer service to smaller areas.

ITU is the abbreviation for "International Telecommunication Union."

Java is the technology that is used to create active Web pages. Java was developed by Sun Microsystems, Incorporated. (Also see **Applet**.)

KBPS (Kilo Bits Per Second) is a measure of the rate of data transmission equal to 1,000 bps.

LAN is the abbreviation for "Local Area Network."

LISTSERV (*electronic mailing* LIST SERV*er*) is a program maintaining lists of e-mail addresses. A user can request that LISTSERV add their e-mail address to a list or delete it.

Login is entering an account identifier and password to access a timesharing computer.

Long-Haul Network is a synonym for Wide Area Network.

Mailbox is a storage area on disk, holding incoming e-mail messages until a user reads the mail.

Mail Exploder is a program that accepts e-mail messages, and then sends a copy of the message to each recipient on a list.

MBPS (Millions of Bits Per Second) is a measure of the rate of data transmission equal to one million bps.

MIME is the abbreviation for "Multipurpose Internet Mail Extensions."

Modem (MO*dulator*/DEM*odulator*) is a device used to transmit digital data a long distance across an analog transmission path.

Moderated Newsgroup is a netnews discussion group. Each submission is sent to someone who edits it before sending the memo to the newsgroup.

Modulation is the electronic data encoded in a modem for transmission.

Modulator is the electronic device in a modem encoding data for transmission.

Mosaic is a single computer program providing an interface to the Internet, gopher, and other services.

Multicast is the technique used to send a file to a selected set of other computers.

Multimedia is a term describing any display text, graphics, images, and sounds.

Netiquette is a list of suggestions for how to behave when using the Internet.

Netnews is the abbreviation for network news.

Netscape is a company that sells an Internet bulletin board service.

News Article is a message that appears on a bulletin board in the network news service.

Newsgroup is a single bulletin board in the network news service. A single user can subscribe to multiple newsgroups.

NFS (Network File System) is service that lets computers access each other's file systems. The difference between NFS and **FTP** is that NFS accesses pieces of a file as needed without copying the entire file.

NII is the abbreviation for "National Information Infrastructure."

Open System is a nonproprietary technology or system that any manufacturer can use. An open system connects systems to other systems that normally couldn't work together.

Packet is used informally to describe a unit of data sent across a packet switching network.

Password is the secret code a user enters to gain access to a time-sharing system.

Ph is the name of the client program used with the **qi** information service. Ph provides information about an individual.

PING (Packet InterNet Groper) is the name of a program used with TCP/IP internets to test. Ping sends the computer a file and waits for a reply.

Plugin is the technology in which a browser can load additional software allowing the browser to interpret new or alternative data formats.

Point-and-Click Interface is a style of interacting with a computer that uses a mouse instead of a keyboard. The user moves the mouse to position the cursor, and presses a button on the mouse to select the item under the cursor.

Point-to-Point Protocol (PPP) is a protocol used to send TCP/IP traffic across a serial transmission line.

PPP is an abbreviation for Point-to-Point Protocol.

Protocol are the rules two or more computers must follow to exchange messages.

PTT is the Abbreviation for "Post, Telegraph, and Telephone."

Public Files are files available to any Internet user.

Public Mailing List is an electronic mailing list letting anyone add themselves, delete themselves, or send a memo.

Qi is the name of the server accessed by the **ph** program.

Real Audio is a technology used to send audio across the Internet.

Remote Login is a service allowing a user on one computer to connect their keyboard and display to a remote computer and run programs.

Request For Comments (RFC) is a series of notes containing the TCP/IP protocol standards and related documents.

RFC is the abbreviation for "Request For Comments."

Route is a route is the path that network traffic takes from its source to its destination.

Router is a special computer that attaches to two or more networks and routes IP datagrams from one to the other.

Search Engine is a term applied to automated search services. The term refers to computer programs that such services use to scan the Internet.

Search Key is a string of characters providing a search service. The service searches for titles or files that contain the string.

Search Tool is a program that lets a user find the location of specific information.

Serial Line IP (SLIP) is a protocol permitting a computer to use TCP/IP over a serial communication medium.

Server is a program that offers a service. Many computers on the Internet run servers to offer services.

SLIP is the abbreviation for "Serial Line IP."

Smiley is a sequence of characters, found in an e-mail message, that indicates humorous intent.

Stack is a term that refers to all the TCP/IP software on a computer. This term is derived from the way software is organized internally.

Surfing the Internet is a slang term that means using Internet services to browse information.

Talk is a program that allows two people to communicate with each other using keyboards and display screens. Each person's screen is divided in half; one half shows what the user types, while the other half shows what the other person types.

TCP is the abbreviation for "Transmission Control Protocol."

TCP/IP is the name of protocols that specify how computers communicate on the Internet.

TELNET is the Internet remote login service. TELNET lets a user at one site interact with a remote timesharing system at another site.

Text File is any file of textual characters separated into lines. Text files on the Internet use the **ASCII** character encoding.

Textual Interface is a style of interacting with a computer using a keyboard. Keystrokes are entered and the computer responds.

Token Ring is a type of Local Area Network (**LAN**) which the network passes from computer to computer in a complete cycle.

Traceroute is a program that lets a user find the path a file will take as it crosses the Internet to a specific destination.

Transmission Control Protocol (TCP) is one of the two major TCP/IP protocols. TCP handles the difficult task of ensuring that all data arrives at the destination in the correct order. The term often refers to software that implements the TCP standard.

Traveling the Information Superhighway is a phrase used by the public that means using Internet services to browse information.

Trickle is a service that provides electronic mail access to FTP. A user ends an e-mail message to a trickle server; the server reads the message, obtains a copy of the file, and transmits an e-mail reply that contains the copy.

Unicast is the technique for sending a file through the Internet from a single source to a single destination.

Uniform Resource Locator (URL) is a short character string used by browsers to identify a particular page of information on the Internet.

UNIX is a computer operating system developed at AT&T Bell Laboratories.

URL is the abbreviation for "Uniform Resource Locator."

USENET is a group of computers exchanging network news.

UUCP (UNIX to UNIX Copy Program) is software that allows one computer to copy files from another.

Video Teleconference Service allows a group of users to exchange video information over the Internet.

Virtual Network is used to refer to the appearance of a single, seamless network system.

WAIS is the abbreviation for "Wide Area Information Server."

WAN is the abbreviation for "Wide Area Network."

Web Site is a computer attached to the Internet which runs on a Web server that makes a set of Web pages available to browsers.

Whiteboard Service is a service that allows a group to establish a session that permits all of them to see and modify the same display.

Wide Area Information Server (WAIS) is an Internet automated search service that locates documents containing key words or phrases.

Wide Area Network (WAN) is network technology spanning large geographic distances.

Window is a rectangular area on a screen devoted to one particular application program. Windows can overlap and can be moved on top of other windows.

World Wide Web (WWW) is an Internet service that organizes information using hypermedia.

WWW is the abbreviation for "World Wide Web."

CHAPTER 21

THE GRAPHIC DESIGN
TRADE CUSTOMS

Simply put, "Trade Customs" are the general terms and
conditions for sales within the graphic design and printing
industries. Trade Customs, however, are not contracts.
They can always be circumvented in part or whole by an agreement between you, the client, and/or the printer.

The Graphic Design Trade Customs*

There have been many attempts at setting standards for the
graphic design industry. The Graphic Artists Guild has developed
a Code of Ethics, which is meant to define the design company's
responsibilities as well as the client's. These ethics are very good,
and are in no way contradicted by the Trade Customs, which are
aimed specifically at the business side of design.

There are many contracts used by design firms. Your own
company may have a standard contract. The Graphic Design
Trade Customs can be used in conjunction with any contract as
long as it doesn't contradict that document.

The American Institute of Graphic Arts (AIGA) has also
published a Code of Ethics, as well as a standard contract for
graphic designers.

---

*The Graphic Design Trade Customs are printed in their entirety on pages
189–192.

The problem with the AIGA contract is that it covers so much detail it can scare off your potential client. I feel this contract is viable for very large projects, but for small- to medium-sized projects, the AIGA contract may be overkill. There are many projects that will come in and go out so fast that there is only time for a memo.

Other graphic design professional organizations have published guidelines for writing contracts to protect the design company from all of the pitfalls a complicated project can produce. These guidelines are very helpful and should not be dismissed. A contract usually applies to one specific project and further defines the responsibilities of both parties, including scope of work, the schedule, the costs, and terms of payment. A contract is always a good idea. It may be no more than a letter of agreement between you and the client, but the rule of thumb is to cover your bottom line. The bigger the bottom line, the more paper you need to cover it.

The bigger the bottom line,
the more paper you need
to cover it.

The Graphic Design Trade Customs define specific areas of responsibility between you and the client. They lean toward protecting you because the client has a distinct advantage over the design company. It's the golden rule. "He who has the gold makes the rules." Without the Trade Customs, designers are sometimes at the mercy of their client's ideas and wishes.

Now that designers are in the "Electronic Age," there seems to be a whole new set of problems concerning copyright and ownership of artwork. The Trade Customs address these issues with some very basic common sense. Unless there is another agreement between you and your client, your company owns the reproduction rights of its work.

Be advised that the area of copyright ownership is a subtle one, yet because of recent changes in the law, it promises to be a controversial area that must be addressed. Ever watch *The People's Court* with Judge Judy? It always seems that the party with a piece of paper wins. This is true in life and business as well. When you have established a solid paper trail, chances are you'll prevail in a commonsense dispute. Of course this won't affect someone who is basically dishonest, but then again, nothing will.

Why Do Designers Have Trade Customs?

When you and the client or a printer agree on the production of a work, you may not realize that the simple contract you sign carries a host of terms and conditions you neither intended nor realized were present. In almost every state there are laws grouped under a heading generically referred to as the Uniform Commercial Code (U.C.C.). The Code is a compilation of laws that address routine commercial transactions such as the formation of the agreement, the inclusion of terms and conditions, warranties that are made (or more often not made), and many other factors.

The U.C.C. is intended to apply only to the sale of goods, but it is such a comprehensive work that courts tend to use it more widely. While designers may well consider themselves in the service business, designers do in fact deliver a product or "good." As a result, the U.C.C. could well be used (usually at the urging of a disgruntled client) to interpret the simple "contract" signed by design company and client. One example of the U.C.C.'s applicability to a standard contract could be the automatic inclusion of a warranty that the product is fit for the specific and particular purpose the client described to the design company.

While the U.C.C. is not our focus here, it highlights the importance of crafting a clear statement of rights and responsibilities between design company and client and of clearly understanding the industry norm. When there is a dispute, the U.C.C. guides a court in determining the rights and obligations of parties to an agreement. In cases where the parties have previously worked with each other, the court will look to this prior "course of dealing," to help determine what the parties knew and reasonably could have expected out of their relationship.

---

*It pays for you
not to bury the Trade Customs
like some fine print in a
real estate contract.*

If there is no track record, the court will look to "the standard usage of trade." In effect, the focus shifts from the particular parties to what others in the industry do and have done in similar situations. It is the U.C.C.'s instruction to "look to the industry" that makes trade customs so important.

If an industry develops, harmonizes, and widely disseminates terms and conditions governing the dealings of its participants, it is only reasonable that a court look to these understandings for guidance in a particular dispute. It was with this understanding that the Trade Customs were drafted. The goal is to promote harmonious relations through well understood and clearly explained terms and conditions. Parties with knowledge of what is expected and obligated, as opposed to what is merely desired and sought, will always be better off; the Trade Customs eliminate the confusion over terms that lie at the heart of so many simple business disputes. Therefore, in order to work with designers, you should understand the Trade Customs and their implications.

How and Why Were the Trade Customs Developed?

The Trade Customs were developed for the Art Director's Club of Metropolitan Washington and later edited for the International Design by Electronics Association to include the new computer technology.

The Trade Customs address responsibilities of both you and

the client which are not spelled out in a commercial agreement between you. Any of the Trade Customs that are altered by an agreement between the two of you and your client will no longer be in force. For example, some companies issue purchase orders to designers that contradict certain parts of the Trade Customs. If you do not formally disagree with the client's purchase order, the client can rightfully claim that that Trade Custom does not apply. This is another good reason for you to make sure your client has a copy of the Trade Customs as soon as possible.

What Do the Trade Customs Mean to Me?

Let's look at each part of the Trade Customs and to see what they mean to you, your company, and your client. Some of these terms have been covered earlier in this book. They should now be read for their part in the overall trade customs and for their relationships to one another.

These Trade Customs are worded so that they can be easily understood. You should still be sure you know what the words mean.

1. Estimate

An estimate is a "best guess" as to what it will cost for the design company to produce a project. Estimates are usually offered when there are still some unknowns, but you need to give some idea of cost for a budget. It is important for you to make it clear that the estimate is not a fixed price bid or proposal, and to clearly spell out what elements are not included in the estimate. Common sense tells us there is no such thing as a "ball park estimate." The price you give should be carefully thought out to cover the worst-case scenario, but since there usually are some unknowns, an estimate is an educated guess. I've learned that most people treat an estimate as though it's carved in granite. Don't make this same mistake. An estimate is a "guess-timate." A quote is just the opposite. Estimates are for loose budgeting and they can vary from reality by the extent of unknown variables. Don't get the two mixed up.

2. Quotation

A quotation is a fixed price for producing a project. Generally, a quotation includes costs for all facets of the job. If there is any work not defined in the specifications, you should assign an hourly rate to this work and note it in the quotation as such. If any materials or out-of-pocket expenses, such as travel, food, lodging, etc., are not included, these areas should also be clearly stated in the quotation.

Because the cost of labor and materials may change, quotations are subject to acceptance within thirty days. This time frame can be altered if you and the client agree to change it. Quotations do not usually include author's alterations or changes by the client because each company has a different approval process and a different way of organizing its work. Sales tax is not included in a quotation unless the client and design company agree to include it.

3. Alterations

Alteration charges apply to changes the client makes after your company has produced the work initially agreed upon by both parties. You should make it very clear to the client what constitutes alterations, such as how many layouts will be shown for what amount of money. The client's concept of alterations may differ from yours, so the best course is for you to write a memorandum to the client as to when alterations begin. It can be very dangerous and costly to try to explain these things later.

4. Overtime

On the surface, overtime seems very simple and straightforward. However, there are pitfalls. First, the client should be informed that their change in the previously agreed upon schedule has made overtime necessary. Second, the client should know what your company's overtime rate is, and if at all possible, how much overtime will be needed. On the other hand, if overtime is contemplated from the beginning, the client should let you know if this is part of their production requirements.

Overtime differs by design company. Some feel their hourly rate does not need to increase because they work late hours on many projects anyway. Others feel that the client should pay a premium for schedule changes that cause overtime.

5. Copyright/Ownership

Your design company's work is automatically protected under federal copyright law. Until the design company agrees to transfer copyright ownership (as compared to merely handing over a copy of the work itself), the designer owns all copyrights to his or her work and decides what compensation he or she wants for the reuse of the work. Designers hold the rights to their work, even if the clients beat them to the copyright office and try to register the copyright for themselves!

These principles also apply to designs produced electronically on a computer. Although a design is easy to reuse electronically, or even alter and then reproduce, the design company's rights remain the same. If the client issues a purchase order prior to the start of a project, claiming it is policy that all designs produced for the company belong to the company, the designers may have to relinquish their rights to the work. That is if these terms and conditions have been accepted, and the client seeks a copyright assignment. If the client issues a purchase order *after* the project is completed, the designers can determine if they wish to comply with these terms. If they decide not to comply, the Trade Customs are on their side.

6. Experimental Work

Experimental work, done by the design company at the client's request, is billable. If a design company develops a design for the client without authorization, the work is not billable unless they agree otherwise. This should not be confused with spec work, which is totally against the Trade Customs and most design codes of ethics. Experimental work is usually exempt from sales tax, as it usually is pure labor. It's best to find out if your state considers this work taxable.

7. Condition of Copy

If the client has stated that the final copy for a project will be submitted in a certain manner (such as on paper or disk) and you have given a quotation based on this information, you have the right to amend the quotation if the specifications change. Similarly, if the scope of work has increased because the copy has changed in volume, you should amend the quotation.

8. Production Schedules

Common sense dictates that production schedules established between the client and the design company should not contain any liability factors for either of the parties if the schedule changes because of uncontrollable circumstances, or "acts of God." This can be superceded by a written contract between the client and the design company.

If, on the other hand, the production schedule is delayed due to the client's company review process, the time needed for the design company to complete the project should be increased in direct proportion to the extra time that the client has used.

9. Client's Property

The design company should maintain adequate insurance to cover the client's property while in the design company's possession, unless that property is extraordinarily valuable. If the client's property is unusually valuable, it is their responsibility to notify the design company and to appropriately insure the property. The design company's liability cannot exceed the amount recoverable from their insurance.

10. Outright Purchase vs. Reproduction Rights

Outright purchase gives your client complete copyright ownership and reuse of your company's work. This should be done in writing and worded very carefully, with specific work listed, to avoid later confusion about the extent and amount of work your client purchased. It should be clear that the work can't be altered, if that's your company's policy. This is necessary because of the widespread availability of electronic manipulation.

11. Reuse and Extended Use of Artwork, Disks, or Negatives

Artwork, disks, or negatives should not to be reused or adapted for other purposes without compensation or permission from the designer who created the original. Changing the artwork does not diminish the designer's ownership of it.

If you want to reuse the work or change it, and you do not own all copyrights in the work, the designer who originated the work should be used. If the designer still owns the copyright and the artwork, disk, or negatives need updating, the original designer still owns the designs, and must authorize all further uses of the work.

12. Markups

All of the designer's out-of-pocket or direct expenses are subject to a markup, or handling charge. Expenses subject to markups include: photography, printing, illustration, advertising space, and special supplies/materials purchased for a specific project.

Markups are handling fees and should be discussed and agreed upon by you and the designer.

13. Speculation

Design companies should not be asked to perform work on speculation. In a typical scenario, a client will ask three design firms or individuals to submit a design with a proposal. This might seem harmless on the surface, but if this becomes the rule and not the exception, two thirds of design companies will be doing free work. The simplest answer is to remember that speculative work is against the Trade Customs. Offering a project overview within a proposal is not considered speculative work. It is more of a sign that the design company understands the project's scope and objectives.

14. Terms

As in any business, the design company should ask the client for a purchase order prior to starting work. The purchase order should state the agreed-upon price, terms (such as "net thirty days"), and a production schedule.

If the client cannot issue a purchase order, you should send a memorandum or letter of agreement detailing the same information that would be contained in the purchase order. You do not have to have the client sign this letter if it says, "If any of the information contained in this (memo or letter) is incorrect, please notify (your name) in writing and/or by fax within twenty-four hours." Once again, a paper trail will protect you.

If the client disputes your company's invoice, Trade Customs states that the dispute should be made in writing and submitted to the design company within fifteen days after receipt of the invoice. It is not uncommon for a client to dispute an invoice when it is ninety days old and everyone's memory is a little foggy.

If there is a dispute over part of an invoice, the client should remit the amount not in dispute within the terms of your company's invoice and handle the disputed portion as a separate transaction.

15. Liability

The design company is only liable for the correction of errors made by the company. The ultimate proofing responsibility rests with the client. This was established by printers years ago. It is only common sense that because of the nature of technical jargon, whether it's medical, legal, or scientific, the client must be responsible for their own proofing.

If the design company is asked to approve a printer's proof because the client cannot be available, the design company should have the client sign a letter of agreement releasing the design company from any liability because of an error in proofing. If your design company is purchasing the printing and signs off on the printer's blueline, your design company may be liable if there is a mistake in the printed piece.

As in the Typographers Trade Customs, proofreading is the client's responsibility. Correcting an error is the design company's responsibility and should be done free of charge to the client. The Graphic Design Trade Customs state that in any instance, the design company is not liable for more than the design and production fees of a project.

16. Indemnification

This sounds complicated, but the definition is not as intimidating as the word itself. It simply means that the design company is protected from liability if they unknowingly create a design that is already in use, copyrighted, or trademarked. The key word is "unknowingly." Anyone can accidentally design something that is in use somewhere else (and this does not constitute copyright infringement). Your client has the responsibility (as well as the legal obligation) to institute a trademark search for any word or logo design. Nothing should be produced with the new mark on it until a thorough search has been made.

The client should be sure that all materials furnished to the design company are free and clear of any copyright or trademark problems. If the client fails to obtain correct usage rights, the client, not the design company, is liable.

If the client makes false statements or plagiarizes within copy submitted to the design company, the client, not the design company, is responsible for any legal repercussions and accepts all liability.

17. Print Management/Press Inspections

If your company offers to press inspect a project, the client's responsibility for final proofreading remains in effect. The client is responsible for signing off on the blueline. The design company is responsible for signing off on a press proof for color only. The color must be acceptable by industry standards. The printer is responsible for ensuring the remainder of the press run is consistent with the approved press proof.

Clients should be allowed to attend a press inspection. They will gain a different perspective of proofing and will be present to participate in the final okay for color.

What If There Is a Dispute?

The Graphic Design and Printing Trade Customs are terms and conditions of sales. They state what the design and printing industries consider common practice. It is a statement of how they do business. If your or your client's policies differ, it is best to get this out, up front.

The Graphic Design Trade Customs are printed in their entirety on the following pages.

The Graphic Design Trade Customs

The Graphic Design Trade Customs were developed by Don Sparkman for the International Design by Electronics Association, the Graphic Artists Guild, and the Art Director's Club of Metropolitan Washington. They have been adopted by the graphic design industry and reflect the current laws and practices of design professionals.

Trade Customs are those practices which delineate the specific areas of responsibility with regard to a special trade or operation which might not be outlined in a commercial agreement. Where a commercial agreement is silent with regard to one or more practices, the Trade Customs areas are used to interpret the intent of the parties. It should be clearly understood that the Trade Customs protect both parties in a commercial agreement. It is, therefore, the responsibility and obligation of involved parties to understand their content and meaning.

1. Estimate: (A preliminary projection of cost which is not intended to be binding.) Estimates are based upon prevailing wages, the anticipated hours of work, and cost of materials and supplies necessary to produce work in accordance with preliminary copy, style, and specifications and are not binding upon the designer unless a firm quotation has been issued.

2. Quotation: A quotation is a fixed price for producing a given project. A quotation is firm unless otherwise specified. Quotations are subject to acceptance within thirty (30) days and are based on the cost of labor and materials on the date of the quote. If changes occur in the cost of materials, labor, or other costs prior to acceptance, the right is reserved to change the price quote. Subsequent projects will be subject to price revision if required. Quotations do not include alterations or applicable sales tax unless otherwise specified.

3. Alterations: Alteration charges are incurred by a client when a change is made to: approved layout, approved manuscript, mechanicals or disk produced correctly, or any new work not within the original specifications.

4. Overtime: Overtime is work performed by the designer in excess of the work schedule of the project. Overtime may be charged at the designer's prevailing rates for this service.

5. Copyright/Ownership: Creative work such as sketches, illustrations, layouts, designs, icons, logos, etc. produced on paper, computer disks, or any other medium are protected under the 1976 Copyright Act. Until the designer transfers ownership rights, creative work remains the property of the designer. There can be no use of the designer's work except upon compensation to be determined by the designer. Purchase orders issued after the completion of creative work, claiming the client's ownership of creative work, are not valid unless agreed upon by both parties.

6. Experimental Work: Experimental or preliminary work performed at the client's request will be charged at current rates and may not be used by the client until the designer has been reimbursed in full for the work performed. All experimental work performed by a designer without authorization of the client is not billable.

7. Condition of Copy: If original copy, disk or manuscript, furnished by the client to the designer differs from that which was originally described and consequently quoted, the original quotation shall be amended or a new quotation will be issued.

8. Production Schedules: Production schedules will be established and adhered to by client and designer, provided that neither shall incur any liability or penalty for delays due to state of war, riot, civil disorder, fire, labor trouble, strikes, accidents, energy failure, equipment breakdown, delays of suppliers or carriers, action of government or civil authority, acts of God, or other causes beyond the control of client or designer. Where production schedules are not adhered to by the client, final delivery date(s) will be subject to renegotiation.

9. Client's Property: The designer will maintain fire, extended coverage, vandalism, malicious mischief, and sprinkler leakage insurance covering all property belonging to the client while such property is in designer's possession. The designer's liability for such property shall not exceed the amount recoverable from such insurance. Client's property of extraordinary value shall be specially protected, only if the client identifies the property as requiring extraordinary coverage.

10. Outright Purchase Versus Reproduction Rights: These terms should be established at the time of purchase. Outright purchase gives the buyer physical possession of the artwork, disk, or negatives, while reproduction rights and related copyright interests require the return of the original to the artist. Outright purchase does not give to the buyer commercial or private reproduction rights or any other copyright interests unless so stipulated in the purchase agreement. The matter of first reproduction rights with subsequent reproduction rights subject to additional compensation should be clearly understood at the time of purchase.

11. Reuse and Extended Use of Artwork, Disks, or Negatives: Artwork, disks, or negatives purchased for a specific use cannot be reused or adapted for other purposes than originally planned without additional compensation to the artist. If this possibility exists at the time of purchase, it should be so stated and the price adjusted accordingly. If reuse or adaptation occurs after purchase, the buyer should negotiate reasonable additional compensation with the artist. Whenever adaptation requires the services of an artist, and the creator has performed to the buyer's satisfaction, the artist should be given the opportunity to revise his or her own work.

12. Markups: Any services or goods such as typography, printing, photography, etc., or materials used specifically for the completion of a given project will be billed to the client with an appropriate markup. This markup is a handling fee only and, unless otherwise agreed, does not include any professional or management fees.

13. Speculation: Graphic designs should not be asked for on speculation by a client. Design contests, except for educational or philanthropic purposes, are also considered speculation.

14. Terms: By assigning an order verbally, in writing, or by purchase order, the client agrees to the designer's terms of payment and late charges on unpaid balances. Payment shall be whatever was set forth in quotation or invoice unless otherwise provided in writing. Disputes over invoices must be made by the client in writing within a period of fifteen (15) days after the client's receipt of the invoice in question. Failure to make such claim within the stated period shall constitute acceptance and an admission that the client agrees with the invoice submitted. If only a portion of the invoice is in dispute, it is the client's responsibility to pay the portion not in dispute within the terms of the invoice.

15. Liability: A designer is only liable for the correction of errors made during the design and mechanical processes. The ultimate proofing prior to printing is always the client's responsibility unless the designer accepts this responsibility in written agreement. In any instance, the designer cannot be liable for more than the design and mechanical costs of a job in dispute.

16. Indemnification: The client shall indemnify and hold harmless the designer from any and all losses, costs, expenses, and damages (including court costs and reasonable attorney fees) on account of any and all manner of claims, demands, actions, and proceedings that may be instituted against the designer on grounds alleging that the said designer unknowingly violated any copyrights or any proprietary right of any person. Any materials such as photographs, photostats, transparencies, drawings, paintings, maps, diagrams, etc. furnished by the client to the designer should be free and clear of any copyright or trademark infringements. The designer is indemnified against any liability pursuant to the client's failure to obtain correct usage rights of said materials. Any false statements knowingly or unknowingly given to the designer, by the client, to be used as factual information to promote a product or service shall remain the client's sole responsibility for substantiation. The designer is indemnified from any liability due to the client's negligence.

17. Print Management/Press Inspections: If a designer performs a press inspection for a client, the client's responsibility for proofing remains in effect. If the client has signed a printer's blueline, the designer is not responsible for any errors reflected in the approved blueline. If the designer approves color on a press proof or any other color proof, the designer is only responsible for approving color acceptable by industry standards. The printer is responsible for ensuring that the subsequent press run matches the color within acceptable standards of the proof approved by the designer.

The Graphic Design Trade Customs can vary from one design firm to another. It is important to include what is important to your company. As I mentioned earlier, these are just terms of conditions for sales, and the client always has the right to issue their own terms. But this must be done up-front, not when the project is completed.

For a free copy of the Graphic Design Trade Customs on Macintosh disk write to:

Graphic Design Trade Customs
Sparkman + Associates, Inc.
1025 Connecticut Avenue, N.W.
Suite 1201
Washington, DC 20036

Include $6.00 for shipping and handling.

CHAPTER 22

THE PRINTING INDUSTRY TRADE CUSTOMS

The Printing Trade Customs* are similar to the Graphic Design Trade Customs. They are usually printed on the reverse side of a printer's estimate sheet. If you receive a printer's estimate by fax, read the front to see if there is a reference to information printed on the reverse side. This is a good idea with any fax. Lease agreements almost always have terms printed on the reverse side.

The printing industry depends on the Trade Customs to ensure their position in areas of liability. You must read them and understand their magnitude. Printers usually have more at stake than graphic designers because of their overhead. They purchase paper and this alone can be a large financial liability if a printing job is rejected.

You need to know what these Trade Customs mean even if your client is buying the printing. You are the consultant and to be effective, your client must rely on you for all the answers. You may also have to assume some liability when performing print management. It's easy to get caught in the middle when you are working with a printer. These are the terms and conditions that printers work under.

---

*The Printing Trade Customs are printed in their entirety on pages 199–202.

You Have Rights

You can disagree with any portion of the Printing Trade Customs, as long as you do it in advance and the printer agrees. Your best way to change the terms of the printer's Trade Customs is to state your own and have the printer agree in writing.

Your Purchase Order Can Be Your Trade Customs

You should always issue a purchase order when starting a printing project. And no project is too small.

On your purchase order you should reference the way your company does business. If you feel the negatives or any materials generated by the printer belong to you, this should be stated clearly on your PO. If you disagree with overruns and underruns, this should also be stated. The key phrase to this is, "Upon acceptance of this purchase order, you (the printer) agree to my terms and conditions as stated within this written order."

Let's look at the Printing Trade Customs and what they mean in the areas of responsibility on your part as well as the printer's. Once again, you will see these customs are weighted in the printer's favor. Now is the time to formulate your own set of rules to be incorporated in that new purchase order you are composing.

1. Quotation

A quotation is a fixed price and is only good for sixty days. The quote is based on current material costs. Quotations can vary by what is included in the total price versus separate costs for halftones, color separations, etc. Make sure each quote gives a true bottom line.

2. Orders

Orders, verbal or written, cannot be cancelled without some compensation to the printer if expenses have been incurred.

194

3. Experimental Work

Experimental work produced by the printer remains the printer's property. This is superceded if *you've paid for the work*. If you or your client are billed for experimental work, discuss ownership of materials.

4. Creative Work

Any creative work done by the printer, such as layouts, artwork, and the like, remains the property of the printer. If this is contrary to your wishes, I suggest you include an amendment in your purchase order stating that all creative work belongs to you or your company. Remember, everything is negotiable.

5. Condition of Copy

This parallels the Graphic Design Trade Customs in as much as the copy should be the same as that which the quote was based upon. If it is a manuscript, it should be prepared in a clean professional manner. If not, expect extra charges.

6. Preparatory Materials

Preparatory materials are treated the same as items 3 and 4. They are the property of the printer. Once again, you may want to revisit this in your purchase order.

7. Alterations

Alterations or change orders are billable. This is an area where you can control costs. It is also a profit center for most printers because customers are often careless during the proofing stages.

8. Prepress Proofs

Prepress proofs are a printer's bible. You must treat them the same way. Always make a photocopy of any proof you sign. If you mark "OK with corrections," it is still your responsibility to make sure the printer made the corrections. In this age of fax machines, there should be a way for you to sign off one last time. If in doubt, press inspect the job and remember, the first thing you do on a press inspection is to check the final (blueline) corrections to make sure every one of them has been made. When you assume anything, you are leaving your fate in someone else's hands.

9. Press Proofs

Press Proofs are not usually included in the printer's estimate or quote. They are expensive and for most jobs, unnecessary. The new digital proofs are excellent and show you fairly accurate color. Once again, you should press inspect your job at the time of make-ready. If you want to see a press proof, make sure the proof is pulled on the same paper the final job will be printed on. If the printer has not purchased all of the paper for the job, try some different sheets while running the press proofs. This will give you some different options. I especially recommend that you do this whenever you've chosen an uncoated sheet.

10. Color Proofing

This paragraph of the Trade Customs simply gives the printer some wiggle room in matching color. It's up to you to ensure the quality of your work. Here again the best solution is for you to be on press at the time your job is run. Press inspections are the only way to ensure exact color. I recommend taking your client along for a color okay. They agreed on and thus chose the colors when you made the presentation.

Here again, the new digital proofs are great for instantly seeing color problems, and because the information is still in digital form, corrections are much less expensive than the conventional proofs pulled from the final film. Also, digital proofs are perfect for checking the results of system retouching.

196

11. Overruns and Underruns

Overruns and underruns can be up to 10 percent either way. If you must yield a number of copies, you may want to increase your order to ensure you receive the quantity you need. This is not only true with printing, but also speciality items like three-ring binders, cassette cases, etc. And with speciality items you will be charged for the overs. This gets tricky, so make sure you understand your agreement with your vendor.

12. Customer's Property

This paragraph is similar to that of the Graphic Design Trade Customs. It states that the printer will maintain reasonable insurance. If your property exceeds the amount recoverable from the printer's insurance, it's up to you to get more insurance.

13. Delivery

The printer will make local deliveries within the quoted price. If there are special delivery needs, these will be billed as a separate cost to you. The printer will keep accurate and reasonable records. You should do the same.

14. Production Schedules

Production schedules are a two-way street. The printer is not responsible for an interruption due to equipment failure, war, acts of God, etc. This is fairly typical. After all, these same things can affect you.

Most printers will not commit to a firm schedule until you or your client has signed off on the blueline.

15. Customer Furnished Materials

This means any materials you supply to the printer should be produced to the printer's specifications. If they are not, you will be billed accordingly. In the electronic age, it's best to meet with the printer and discuss his prepress requirements.

16. Terms

The printer requires total payment as set forth in the proposal, quote, or bid. If there is a dispute, it must be filed in writing within fifteen days of delivery of the printed job. If you or your client has no local credit history, cash up front or C.O.D. may be required.

17. Liability

The printer isn't liable for any amount exceeding the cost of the printed job. This covers profits lost by you or your company. In the event you have not paid the printer for past service, your work could be held hostage until you pay what's owed.

18. Indemnification

This frees the printer of any liability due to copyright infringements, untrue statements that you may have made in the copy, or just about any other thing that could happen that is beyond the printer's control. This is very fair with the volume of work most printers produce.

Like the Graphic Design Trade Customs, the printer should print these on the back of their quotations or submit them to you prior to the beginning of the print production process. It is not enough to show you the Trade Customs after they have printed your work and expect you to abide by them. Also, printers may alter the Trade Customs to suit the way they do business. It's best to review each printer's practices before they become an issue.

The following pages have the Printing Trade Customs reprinted in their entirety.

The Printing Trade Customs

Trade Customs have been in general use in the printing industry throughout the United States of America for more than sixty years.

Originally formally promulgated, Annual Convention, United Typothetae of America, 1922.

Revised, updated, and repromulgated, Annual Convention, Printing Industries of America, Inc., 1945 and 1974.

1. Quotation: A quotation not accepted within sixty (60) days is subject to review. All prices are based on material costs at the time of quotation.

2. Orders: Orders regularly placed, verbal or written, cannot be cancelled except upon request that will compensate printer against loss incurred in reliance of that order.

3. Experimental Work: Experimental or preliminary work performed at the customer's request will be charged for at the current rates and may not be used until the printer has been reimbursed in full for the amount of the charges.

4. Creative Work: Creative work such as sketches, copy, dummies, and all preparatory work developed and furnished by the printer, shall remain his exclusive property and no use of the same shall be made, nor any ideas obtained therefrom be used, except upon compensation to be determined by the printer, and not expressly identified and included in the selling price.

5. Conditions of Copy: Upon receipt of original copy or manuscript, should it be evident that the condition of the copy differs from that which had been originally described and consequently quoted, the original quotation shall be rendered void and a new quotation issued. Original copy or manuscript should be clearly typed, double-spaced on 8½" x 11" uncoated stock, one side only. Condition of copy which deviates from this standard is subject to re-estimating and pricing review by the printer at the time of submission of copy, unless otherwise specified in estimate.

6. Preparatory Materials: Working mechanical art, type, negatives, positives, flats, plates, and other items when supplied by the printer, shall remain his exclusive property unless otherwise agreed in writing.

7. Alterations: Alterations represent work performed in addition to the original specifications. Such additional work shall be charged at current rates and be supported with documentation upon request.

8. Prepress Proofs: Prepress proofs shall be submitted with original copy. Corrections are to be made on "master set," returned marked "OK" or "OK with corrections," and signed by the customer. If revised proofs are desired, request must be made when proofs are returned. Printer cannot be held responsible for errors under any or all of the following conditions: If the work is printed per customer's OK; if changes are communicated verbally; if customer has not ordered proofs; if the customer has failed to return proofs with indications of changes; or if the customer has instructed printer to proceed without submission of proofs.

9. Press Proofs: Unless specifically provided in printer's quotation, press proofs will be charged for at current rates. An inspection sheet of any form can be submitted for customer approval, at no charge, provided customer is available at press during the time of make-ready. Lost press time due to customer delay, or customer changes and corrections, will be charged at current rates

10. Color Proofing: Because of differences in equipment, processing, proofing substrates, paper, inks, pigments, and other conditions between color proofing and production pressroom operations, reasonable variations in color between color proofs, and the completed job shall constitute acceptable delivery.

11. Overruns and Underruns: Overruns or underruns not to exceed 10% on quantities ordered or the percentage agreed upon, shall constitute acceptable delivery. Printer will bill for actual quantity delivered within this tolerance. If the customer requires guaranteed exact quantities, the percentage tolerance must be doubled.

12. Customer's Property: The printer will retain fire, extended coverage, vandalism, malicious mischief, and sprinkler leakage insurance on all property belonging to the customer, while such property is in the printer's possession; printer's liability for such property shall not exceed the amount recoverable from such insurance. Customer's property of extraordinary value shall be insured through mutual agreement.

13. Delivery: Unless otherwise specified, the price quoted is for single shipment, without storage, F.O.B. local customer's place of business or F.O.B. printer's platform for out of town customers. Proposals are based on continuous and uninterrupted delivery of complete order, unless specifications distinctly state otherwise. Charges related to delivery from the customer to the printer, or from customer's suppliers to the printer, are not included in any quotations unless specified. Special priority pickup or delivery service will be provided at current rates upon customer's request. Materials delivered from customer or his suppliers are verified with delivery ticket as to cartons, packages or items shown only. The accuracy of quantities indicated on such tickets cannot be verified and printer cannot accept liability for the shortage based on supplier's tickets. Title for finished work shall pass to the customer upon delivery to carrier at shipping point or upon mailing of invoices for finished work, whichever occurs first.

14. Production Schedules: Production schedules will be established and adhered to by customers and printer, provided that neither shall incur any liability or penalty for delays due to state of war, riot, civil disorder, fire, labor trouble, strikes, accidents, energy failure, equipment breakdown, delays of suppliers or carriers, action of Government or civil authority and acts of God or other causes beyond the control of customer or printer. Where production schedules are not adhered to by the customer, final delivery date(s) will be subject to renegotiation.

15. Customer Furnished Materials: Paper stock, inks, camera copy, film, color separations, and other customer furnished material shall be manufactured, packed, and delivered to printer's specifications. Additional cost due to delays or impaired production caused by specification deficiencies shall be charged to customers.

16. Terms: Payment shall be whatever was set forth in the quotation or invoice unless otherwise provided in writing. Claims for defects, damages or shortages must be made by the customer in writing within a period of fifteen (15) days after delivery of all or any part of the order. Failure to make such claim within the stated period shall constitute irrevocable acceptance and an admission that they fully comply with terms, conditions and specifications.

17. Liability: Printer's liability shall be limited to stated selling price of any defective goods, and shall in no event include special or consequential damages, including profits (or profits lost). As a security for payment of any sum due or to become due under terms of any agreement, printer shall have the right, if necessary, to retain possession of and shall have a lien on all customer property in printer's possession including work in process and finished work. The extension of credit or the acceptance of notes, trade acceptance or guarantee of payment shall not affect such security interest and lien.

18. Indemnification: The customer shall indemnify and hold harmless the printer from any and all loss, cost, expense, and damages (including court costs and reasonable attorney fees) on account of any and all manner of claims, demands, actions, and proceedings that may be instituted against the printer on grounds alleging that the said printing violates any copyrights or any proprietary right of any person, or that it contains any matter that is libelous or obscene or scandalous, or invades any person's right to privacy or other personal rights, except to the extent that the printer contributed to the matter. The customer agrees, at the customer's own expense, to promptly defend and continue the defense of any such claim, demand, action or proceeding that may be brought against the printer, provided that the printer shall promptly notify the customer with respect thereto, and provided further that the printer shall give to the customer such reasonable time as the exigencies of the situation may permit in which to undertake and continue the defense thereof.

Since the Printing Trade Customs can vary from one printer to another, just like the Graphic Design Trade Customs, it is important to read each set. As I mentioned earlier, these are just terms of conditions for sales and you always have the right to issue your own terms. But once again, this must be done upfront, not when the project is completed.

Today more than ever before, electronic files can be manipulated. This means your work, once it's on the printer's system, is no longer under your control. I recommend you reference in your purchase order that you own all rights to your work and that the electronic files must be returned to you. You should also ask that the printer remove your data from his system, unless his retouching is in the files.

WHERE THE CLIENTS ARE

Most design firms work with local accounts because it's easier to call on them as well as serve them. The exception to this rule is when the design company has outgrown its locale or there is not enough business there to support it. A few firms just feel they are national in nature and want nothing but national accounts.

Graphic Design Regional and National Markets

The phone book is often overlooked as a source of companies that are potential design buyers. If a company has a sophisticated ad in the phone book, it's already using a designer. There are also local business directories available in most cities.

Most cities have a business section that appears in their newspaper either weekly or daily. This is an area from which to glean which companies are doing what locally. Their press releases will give you important information to be used in your conversation with their design buyers. In some cities, Dunn and Bradstreet offers lists of companies that are starting up. This may be a gold mine for corporate identity work.

As I mentioned earlier, one of the best ways to reach your local business community is to join one or more of the local groups like the Jaycees, Rotary, Chamber of Commerce, Board of Trade, or even a church. The key is *exposure* and becoming one of the group. Networking is an an art and it should be done naturally. Joining in is better than selling from the outside.

Another way to reach local accounts is to advertise. Too often design firms refuse to advertise in the Yellow Pages, newspapers, or other local publications. They, like doctors and lawyers, feel this is beneath them. Well, we have to face it. We're not doctors or lawyers, and there is a glut of designers in the marketplace. We need an edge, and advertising reaches businesses as well as influential individuals.

There is no way to list all of the local publications and associations in each area of the country. You'll need to do some homework of your own. Don't forget about the printing and paper salespeople in your local area. They can give you leads if they can trust you to protect them with their client, and if you can give them a lead, you'll have more of a chance of them reciprocating.

If you are interested in markets outside your locale, there are many resources available. Remember what we said about the painter earlier. Preparation is 90 percent of the work. The books listed in this section are good sources for anyone wishing to expand his or her marketplace, and that's what selling is all about. No matter how successful a design company becomes, attrition will come into play. Key client contacts will leave a company and their replacements may have their own graphic design companies.

If your company is not looking for more business, it should be looking for replacement business.

General Markets

Artist's & Graphic Designer's Market
Published by: F&W Publications
1507 Dana Avenue
Cincinnati, OH 45207

• This book contains a basic listing of the markets for graphic designers, such as: ad agencies; art publishers and distributors; greeting card, gift item, and paper product companies; magazine publishers; record companies; syndicates; and clip-art companies.

- It also offers: marketing tips for negotiating the best deal, successful self-promotion, business nuts and bolts, and much more.

Corporations

O'Dwyer's Directory of Corporate Communications
Published by: J. R. O'Dwyer Co., Inc.
271 Madison Avenue
New York, NY 10016

(212) 679-2471

- It features basic listings of public relations executives at over two thousand companies and three hundred trade associations.
- It contains a geographic breakdown showing the companies in your area as well as the key decision makers.
- There's a listing of investor-relations officers and employee-communications officers who are the key contacts for annual reports and house organs.
- Also, there's a breakdown of companies in industry groups such as: pharmaceuticals, transportation, healthcare, and many more.

Advertising Agencies

Advertising agencies often buy outside design services. The smaller the agency, the greater the chances are that they are running lean and outsource creative work. Ad agencies are brokers and most of their money is from buying ad space for their clients. Design is a necessary part of the process, but not the profit center.

As a rule, advertising agencies hate overhead. They aren't keen on committing to heavy capital investment on things like computer systems for design. They know how volatile their business is and that they can lose a major account at any time. They can always lay off people, but not computers. If your company is operating state-of-the-art equipment, this could be a big selling point.

It's very important to tailor your portfolio for your client's needs. When approaching an ad agency, don't load your portfolio with annual reports unless that's something they offer their clients. Most agencies have an artist on board, but if they are small to medium their design capabilities are probably limited to a jack of all trades. This means they will need a specialist from time to time.

Your best guide to finding advertising agencies as potential clients is through the:

Standard Directory of Advertising Agencies
Published by: Reed Reference Publishing, Inc.
121 Chanlon Road
New Providence, NJ 07974

(800) 521-8118

- This book contains over three thousand U.S. ad agencies with addresses and telephone numbers, and one thousand foreign agencies.

- There is a geographic cross-reference by state and city giving you regional information.

- The names of senior art directors are included when applicable. The names of art buyers aren't listed, but you will have to call the agency for an appointment and you can get the correct name and title of that person then.

- The agencies' clients are listed. This is key to your selection of work to put in your portfolio.

- Gross billings are given. The size of the agency is indicated by its billings and this indicates their stability.

Publications

Magazines are what I call "evergreen accounts." They are steady buyers of good design. There are exceptions to this rule. If a publication has its own in-house design staff, they may need illustration or photography, but not design. Some publications are run on a shoestring with no budget for good design. Beware.

Trade publications can be very sophisticated as well as award-winners for design excellence. Quite often the more technical the information is in one of these publications, the more fun the designer can have at distilling the dry topics. An example of this is a publication, the *Industrial Launderer*. This magazine is published for just what the title says, industrial launderers. It has also received more awards than any other publication of its type and has even been featured in *Graphis*.

Gebbie Press All-In-One Directory

Published by: Gebbie Press
Box 1000
New Paltz, NY 12561

(914) 255-7560

- This guide contains an alphabetical list of names and addresses of over 7,500 consumer and trade publications, but no phone numbers.

- The above are divided into two hundred well-defined categories.

- There is a separate list of newspaper-distributed magazines with addresses and circulation figures.

Working Press of the Nation, Vol. 2: Internal Publications Directory

Published by: Reed Reference Publishing, Inc.
121 Chanlon Road
New Providence, NJ 07974

(800) 521-8118

- This book contains a basic alphabetical list of names and addresses of the publications of several thousand companies, clubs, groups, and government agencies.

- The industrial categories are cross-referenced, which pinpoints the publications possibly related to your firm's type of work.

- The circulations are cross-referenced, showing quickly which publications would have larger budgets.

Public Relations Firms

There is a significant amount of work given to design firms by public relations companies. Annual reports can often be a shared project. Public relations companies often share the advertising agencies' fear of too much overhead. Some of the very large firms have a designer or designers on staff, but this is a rarity.

O'Dwyer's Directory of Public Relations Firms
Published by: J. R. O'Dwyer Co., Inc.
271 Madison Avenue
New York, NY 10016

(212) 679-2471

- This book contains over nine hundred public relations firms throughout the United States.

- There is a geographic cross-reference by state and city, giving you regional information.

- The directory includes a list of accounts cross-referenced to over six thousand clients. This will help you to select a public relations company that will best utilize your firm's strengths.

- The size of each public relations firm is listed, indicated by number of employees.

PROFESSIONAL ORGANIZATIONS AND PUBLICATIONS THAT CAN HELP YOU

There are many professional organizations that can help you achieve many things. Some of the benefits are: education, technical support, networking, new product and service information, conferences/seminars, and social contacts.

This appendix lists professional publications that can help you learn more about design trends. There is also a listing of publications that will give you invaluable sources of illustration, stock photography, and live photography.

Design Organizations Are Not Just for Members

You may wish to join the local art directors club in your area, which can give you an inside track on what's happening in your field. If you only want to attend certain meetings featuring speakers you are interested in, you can find a designer who is a member and go as their guest.

Most people don't realize that you don't have to be a member of an organization to get on its mailing list. These groups welcome guests to their meetings. In fact, they openly promote it.

If you are a designer, joining a design group is even more important because you can't afford to become insulated from the latest trends. If you're a buyer of illustration or photography, you'll be kept up to date through club meetings.

Another important benefit of joining an art directors club is the ability to network. This is a great way to meet future employers as well as others who share your interests. Many of the contacts you make will stay with you throughout your career.

If you're selling design now, you could be buying it later. If you can't find a local design group, you can join the following organizations on a national or local level:

American Center for Design (ACD)
325 West Huron Street
Suite 711
Chicago, IL 60610

(800) 257-8657; *www.ac4d.org*

ACD's mission is to educate and inform designers about current research, ideas, and technology. It is a nonprofit national organization serving designers in different fields.

The American Institute of Graphic Arts (AIGA)
164 Fifth Avenue
New York, NY 10010

(212) 807-1990; *www.aiga.org*

The AIGA is involved with the issues of design rather than with the designer. It publishes monthly newsletters, holds conferences and seminars, and presents an annual show of juried design work. AIGA has thirty-five chapters and approximately eighty-five hundred members.

American Society of Media Photographers (ASMP)
Washington Park #502
13 Washington Road
Princeton Junction, NJ 08550

(609) 799-8300

ASMP is a professional organization of photographers. You don't need to join to attend informative meetings on issues ranging from copyrights to the latest techniques in photography.

Art Directors Club of New York
250 Park Avenue South
New York, NY 10003

(212) 674-0500

The Art Directors Club of New York is well known in the "print" community for its annual show. The club's board is made up of some of the greats in design.

Artists Equity Association
3726 Albermarle Street N.W.
Washington, DC 20016

(202) 244-0209

This association deals with issues affecting artists in general. It is a national organization and works with fine artists, protecting their rights.

Artists Equity Association of New York
225 West 34th Street
New York, NY 10001

(212) 736-6480

The association has the same mission as the national one, but operates in the New York metropolitan area.

Association of American Editorial Cartoonists
C/O Jim Lange
Oklahoman
Oklahoma City, OK 73125

(405) 232-3311

The association is concerned with the standards and professional ethics for editorial cartoonists.

Association of Medical Illustrators
6650 N.W. Highway
Suite 112
Chicago, IL 60631

(312) 763-7350

This association is concerned with standards in the practice of medical illustration. This is an excellent source for specialists for legal exhibits. The association promotes its members to the professional world.

Association of Professional Design Firms (APDF)
450 Irwin Street
San Francisco, CA 94107

(415) 626-9774

APDF's role is to ensure the quality of the professional practices of design firm members.

Broadcast Designers Association (BDA)
145 West 45th Street
Suite 1100
New York, NY 10036

(212) 376-6222; *www.bdaweb.com*

BDA is a professional association representing designers in the television/audio and entertainment industries. BDA's issues are on the cutting edge of broadcast design.

Cartoonists Guild
156 West 72nd Street
New York, NY 10023

(212) 873-4023

The guild is concerned with the professional standards of freelance cartoonists and their economic welfare.

Corporate Design Foundation
20 Part Plaza
Suite 321
Boston, MA 02116

(617) 340-7097; *www.cdf.org*

The Corporate Design Foundation is a nonprofit organization serving product, communication, and environmental designers.

The Design Management Institute (DMI)
29 Temple Place
2nd Floor
Boston, MA 02111

(617) 338-6380; *www.dmi.org*

DMI takes a business approach to the management of the design process in large and small companies. DMI is an international force advocating effective design management systems.

Graphic Artists Guild (GAG)
90 John Street
Suite 403
New York, NY 10038-3202

(212) 791-3400

(800) 878-2753; *www.gag.org*

The GAG was formed by artists for artists and is dedicated to protecting their rights and ethical standards. This group is geared to designers rather than buyers.

Industrial Designers Society of America (IDSA)
1142 Walker Road
Great Falls, VA 22066

(703) 759-0100; *www.idsa.org*

IDSA is dedicated to excellence in industrial design and the profession's value to business and government. IDSA is a catalyst between practice and education.

International Association of Business Communicators (IABC)

1 Hallidie Plaza
#600
San Francisco, CA 94102

(415) 782-4635; *www.iabc.com*

IABC is dedicated to effective business communication providing products, services, and activities to organizations so they may achieve excellence in public relations and marketing communication.

International Interactive Communication Society (IICS)

10160 SW Nimbus Avenue
Suite F2
Portland, OR 97223

(503) 620-3604; *www.iics.org*

IICS is an international organization representing multimedia professionals, dedicated to the advancement of the industry.

International Society of Graphic Designers (ISGD)

201 Main Street
Charlestown, MA 02129

(617) 241-7680

ISGD promotes cooperation between U.S. and international graphic designers.

Joint Ethics Committee

P.O. Box 179
Grand Central Station
New York, NY 10017

Joint Ethics Committee arbitrates disputes between graphic designers and their clients. It is sponsored by the Art Directors Club of New York, the American Society of Magazine Photographers, the Graphic Artists Guild, the Society of Illustrators, and the Society of Photographer and Artist Representatives.

National Cartoonists Society (NCS)

9 Ebony Court
Brooklyn, NY 11229

(212) 743-6510

The society represents cartoonists and is an organization for all cartoon disciplines.

National Endowment for the Arts (NEA)

Visual Arts Program
2401 E Street N.W.
Washington, DC 20506

(202) 634-6369

The NEA provides grants for organizations in the arts. NEA has been a political pawn, portrayed by various administrations as an unnecessary agency.

Organization of Black Designers (OBD)

300 M Street S.W.
Suite #N110
Washington, DC 20024

(202) 659-3918; *www.core77.com/OBD*

OBD is a nonprofit national association working to educate the public and design professionals in the importance of contributions by African-Americans and other people of color.

Package Design Council

481 Carlisle Drive
Herndon, VA 22070

(703) 318-7225; *www.packinfo-world.org*

The Package Design Council is a nonprofit organization representing the package design community.

Society for Environmental Graphic Designers (SEGD)
401 F Street N.W.
Suite 333
Washington, DC 20001

(202) 638-5555

SEGD is an international nonprofit society promoting public awareness as well as professional development in environmental graphic design.

Society of Illustrators
128 East 63rd Street
New York, NY 10021

(212) 838-2560

The Society has a rich history of being a forum for some of America's greatest talents. While hosting a national show and producing the *Illustrators Annual*, the Society is also involved in the education side of its art.

Society of Newspaper Design
129 Dryer Street
Providence, RI 02903-3904

(401) 276-2100; *www.snd.org*

SND is an international organization made up of designers, artists, editors, photographers, art directors, students, and faculty involved in newspaper, magazine, and Web page design.

Society of Photographer and Artist Representatives (SPAR)
P.O. Box 845
FDR Station
New York, NY 10150

(212) 628-6492

The society is primarily a New York–based group for reps of artists, photographers, and some designers. It sponsors educational programs for members and representatives just entering the field.

Society of Publication Designers (SPD)
60 East 42nd Street
#721
New York, NY 10165

(212) 983-8585; *www.spd.org*

SPD is a society made up of magazine and newspaper design professionals. SPD promotes the art director's role of a design journalist in the field of publication design.

Type Directors Club (TDC)
60 East 42nd Street
#721
New York, NY 10165

(212) 983-6042; *users.ail.com/typeclub*

TDC is an international club with a membership of designers involved with typography. The club sponsors an annual exhibition and produces a calender of events involving the practice of typography.

Webmaster's Guild
P.O. Box 381231
Cambridge, MA 02238-1231

www.webmaster.org

The Webmaster's Guild represents the many disciplines of developing and supporting Worldwide Web sites. Its goal is the sharing of information in all of the Web disciplines.

There are local chapters of many of the national groups in cities across the United States. I suggest looking in your local phone book to see if there is one near you.

If you decide to join one of these organizations, it is important to remember that you only get out what you put in. This means your optimum return will be the result of working within the organization as a member of a committee. If, on the other hand, you're interested in networking or meeting prospective clients, there are groups that easily afford this, such as the Jaycees, Rotary Clubs, or your industry's trade association.

Professional Publications are Valuable Tools

There are two kinds of publications listed below: magazines that inform you of current design and photographic trends, and source books on stock photography, live photography, illustration, and graphic design.

Whether you live in a metropolitan or a rural area, you will benefit from these publications. Many are free and once you are on their mailing list, you'll receive them on a regular basis. Take advantage of the many free publications available to you.

Professional Publications of Graphic Design

Communication Arts (*CA*)
410 Sherman Avenue
P.O. Box 10300
Palo Alto, CA 94303

(510) 326-6040

Published bimonthly in full color, *CA* features the latest in graphic design trends. The magazine has annuals featuring the best in design and advertising.

Graphic Design USA
1556 Third Avenue
Suite 405
New York, NY 10128

(212) 534-5500

Graphic Design USA is a monthly two-color magazine giving the latest information on design and reporting on who is doing what in the field.

Graphis
141 Lexington Ave.
New York, NY 10016

(212) 532-9387

Graphis is one of the the highest quality full-color publications of its kind. It features graphic design and photography from all over the world.

HOW
P.O. Box 5250
Harlem, IA 51593-0750

(800) 333-1115

HOW magazine is a full-color instructional publication offering design tips and techniques. *HOW* sponsors an annual design conference.

Print
104 Fifth Avenue
New York, NY 10011

(212) 463-0600

Print magazine is bimonthly and features the latest design trends. Printed in full color, with a regional issue each year, this an excellent publication.

Step-By-Step
6000 North Forest Park Drive
P.O. Box 1901
Peoria, IL 61656-1901

(309) 688-2300

Step-By-Step is a full-color publication offering detailed information on design, illustration, and photographic techniques written by professionals in the field.

Source Books for Finding Illustrators and Photographers

This is a basic listing to get you started. There are plenty more and new ones are starting up all the time. These books highlight the work of the various illustrators and photographers, so you can find the styles that appeal to your client or are appropriate for a specific project. Check first to see if there is a fee or commission charged by the publication.

Corporate Showcase
American Showcase
724 Fifth Avenue
New York, NY 10019

(212) 245-0981

This is an illustrated directory of illustrators and photographers. It shows their work and gives you their phone numbers.

Directory of Illustration and Design
P.O. Box 314
Brooklyn, NY 11205

(718) 857-9267

This full-color publication showcases the work of illustrators and designers from all over the United States.

Stock Photography Catalogs

Allstock
222 Dexter Avenue N.
Seattle, WA 98109

(206) 622-6262

This catalog specializes in nature and wildlife photography. The images are mainstream and typical nature shots as well as a mixture of other situations.

The Bettmann Archive
902 Broadway
New York, NY 10010

(212) 614-7240

There is nothing as all-encompassing as Bettman's extensive collection of classic photos, paintings, and other images.

Black Book Stock
Black Book Marketing Group
115 Fifth Avenue
New York, NY 10003

(212) 254-1330

This catalog features stock photography by various photographers with different specialities.

Comstock
Comstock Building
30 Irving Place
New York, NY 10003

(800) 225-2727

This catalog is more "middle of the road" with smiling faces and sunsets.

Direct Stock
10 East 21st Street
14th Floor
New York, NY 10010

(212) 979-6560

Direct Stock also features photography by various photographers, but with a little more flair.

FPG International
32 Union Square East
New York, NY 10003

(212) 777-4210

FPG offers stock photography much in the same vein as Comstock. It's very American, with nothing really experimental.

The Image Bank
111 Fifth Avenue
New York, NY 10003

(212) 539-8300

The Image Bank is general stock photography and it also offers the latest in high-tech special effects.

Masterfile
415 Yonge Street
Suite 200
Toronto, Canada M5b 2E7

(416) 977-7267

Masterfile's catalog also features stock photography by various photographers with different specialities.

Panoramic Images
230 N. Michigan Avenue
Suite 3700
Chicago, IL 60601

(800) 543-5250

This catalog features panoramic views with breathtaking scenes. With the new ways of melding photos within photos, this is a must for those using Photoshop software.

Photonica
141 Fifth Avenue
Suite 8 South
New York, NY 10010

(212) 505-9000

Photonica has one of the most interesting collections of stock images ever assembled. The photography is very contemporary and features images that are illustrations in themselves. This book is the most radical departure from the normal stock photography catalog I have ever seen.

Sharpshooters
4950 Southwest 72 Avenue
Suite 114
Miami, FL 33155

(800) 666-1266

This catalog features interesting stock images of nature, sports, and people in action.

Stock Imagery
711 Kalamath Street
Denver, CO 80204

(800) 288-3686

This book has some interesting stock images. The photography is very crisp and upbeat. There is a good mix of people, family, sports, scenery, and action.

Vintage (Superstock)
New York, NY
Fax (212) 889-9696

San Francisco, CA
Fax (415) 781-9685

Jacksonville, FL
Fax (904) 641-4480

San Francisco, CA
Fax (541) 849-5577

The Vintage series of catalogs feature old photographs from the 1940s to the 1960s. The quality of the images is excellent.

West Stock
2013 Fourth Avenue
Seattle, WA 98121

(206) 728-7726

This is another general catalog featuring mainstream stock photography by various photographers with different specialities.

SELECTED READINGS

American Institute of Graphic Arts. *AIGA Professional Practices in Graphic Design.* New York: Allworth Press, 1998.

Berreswill, Joseph W. *Corporate Design/Graphic Identity Systems.* Glen Cove, N.Y.: International, Inc., 1987.

Black Book Marketing Group. *Black Book Stock.* New York: H. Huntington Stehli, 1993.

Comer, Douglas E. *The Internet Book.* Upper Saddle River, N.J.: Prentice-Hall, Inc., 1997.

Crawford, Tad and Eva Doman Bruck. *Business and Legal Forms for Graphic Designers.* Rev. ed. New York: Allworth Press, 1995.

Dejan, Daniel and others. "Designers Guide to Print Production." *Step-By-Step,* February 1988.

Editorial Committee. *Graphic Artist's Guild Handbook, Pricing & Ethical Guidelines.* New York: Graphic Artists Guild, 1994.

Gold, Ed. *The Business of Graphic Design.* Rev. ed. New York: Watson-Guptill Publications, 1995.

Goldfarb, Roz. *Careers by Design.* New York: Allworth Press, 1993.

Goodman, Danny. *Danny Goodman's Macintosh Handbook.*

New York: Bantam Doubleday Dell, Bantam Books, 1992.

Heller, Steven. *Looking Closer: Critical Writings on Graphic Design*. New York: Allworth Press, 1994.

Heron, Michal and David MacTavish. *Pricing Photography: The Complete Guide to Assignment and Stock Prices*. New York: Allworth Press, 1993.

Herring, Jerry and Mark Fulton. *The Art & Business of Creative Self Promotion*. New York: Watson-Guptill Publications, 1992.

International Paper. *Pocket Pal*. Memphis, Tenn.: International Paper Company, 1992.

Leland, Caryn. *Licensing Art and Design*. Rev. ed. New York: Allworth Press, 1995.

McQuiston, Liz, Barry Kitts, and F.H.F. Henrion. *Graphic Design Source Book*. New York: Chartwell Books, Inc., 1987.

Pederson, Martin. *Graphis Corporate Identity*. Zurich, Switzerland: Graphis Press Corp., 1989.

Supon Design Group. *Using 1, 2 & 3 Colors*. New York: Madison Square Press, 1992.

WHERE TO FIND IT

ABOUT THE AUTHOR

Don Sparkman is the president of his own graphic design firm, Sparkman + Associates, Inc. in Washington, D.C. He founded the company in 1973, and he has personally won numerous awards for design excellence, locally, nationally, and internationally. His firm has developed graphic communications for AT&T, Black and Decker, Cable and Wireless, Coors, Eckerd Drugs, Fortran Communications, GE, Marriott, MCI, Mobil, NASA, Ogilvy & Mather, National Institutes of Health, Rubbermaid, U.S. Postal Service, and many more.

In 1976, Don was selected by the U.S. Bicentennial Committee as one of three designers to judge the design validity of all commemorative items developed for the committee. He is a past president of the Art Directors Club of Metropolitan Washington (ADCMW) and the International Design by Electronics Association (IDEA).

He created the Graphic Design Trade Customs for the ADCMW and IDEA, and has been published in *Step-By-Step* magazine. He has also lectured at the Design Management Institute's National Conference in Martha's Vineyard, George Washington University's Design Center in Washington, D.C., Northern Virginia Community College, the Corcoran School of Art, the American Institute of Graphic Arts, and many other institutions. Sparkman has just published his first fiction novel *The PaperDot-Com,* with Chambers Publishing Group.

Selling Graphic Design was conceived because of Sparkman's acute awareness of the problems encountered by those selling design who have had no formal training. Don has been selling design for his firm for over thirty years, and he knows the tricks of the trade.

In order to keep providing excellent service, Don has immersed his firm in new technologies. In 1985 he bought a Lightspeed computer design system, which was one of the pioneer systems and very powerful for its time. Now, every designer in his firm works on the latest computer design system and is online. Sparkman's e-mail address is *don@sparkmandesign.com.*

While the Internet is an exciting electronic frontier, Sparkman still believes the computer is just another design and communication tool, and that only people are designers. This philosophy has helped him keep his company on the leading edge of technology, while not forgetting why it is there.

Books from Allworth Press

Design Dialogues *by Steven Heller and Elinor Pettit*
(softcover, 6¾ × 10, 272 pages, $18.95)

The Education of a Graphic Designer
edited by Steven Heller (softcover, 6¾ × 10, 256 pages, $18.95)

AIGA Professional Practices in Graphic Design
The American Institute of Graphic Arts, edited by Tad Crawford
(softcover, 6¾ × 10, 320 pages, $24.95)

Design Literacy: Understanding Graphic Design
by Steven Heller and Karen Pomeroy (softcover, 6¾ × 10, 288 pages, $19.95)

**Design Culture: An Anthology of Writing from the AIGA Journal of
Graphic Design** *edited by Steven Heller and Marie Finamore*
(softcover, 6¾ × 10, 320 pages, $19.95)

Looking Closer: Critical Writings on Graphic Design
edited by Michael Bierut, William Drenttel, Steven Heller, and DK Holland
(softcover, 6¾ × 10, 256 pages, $18.95)

Looking Closer 2: Critical Writings on Graphic Design
edited by Michael Bierut, William Drenttel, Steven Heller, and DK Holland
(softcover, 6¾ × 10, 288 pages, $18.95)

Looking Closer 3: Classic Writings on Graphic Design
edited by Michael Bierut, Jessica Helfand, Steven Heller, and Rick Poynor
(softcover, 6¾ × 10, 288 pages, $18.95)

Legal Guide for the Visual Artist, Fourth Edition
by Tad Crawford (softcover, 8½ × 11, 272 pages, $19.95)

Licensing Art and Design, Revised Edition
by Caryn R. Leland (softcover, 6 × 9, 128 pages, $16.95)

**The Copyright Guide: A Friendly Guide for Protecting and Profiting
from Copyrights** *by Lee Wilson* (softcover, 6 × 9, 192 pages, $18.95)

**The Trademark Guide: A Friendly Guide for Protecting and Profiting
from Trademarks** *by Lee Wilson* (softcover, 6 × 9, 192 pages, $18.95)